32.95

C++ Power Paradigms

Other McGraw-Hill Titles of Interest

*For more information about other McGraw-Hill materials,
call 1-800-2-MCGRAW in the United States. In other
countries, call your nearest McGraw-Hill office.*

C++ Power Paradigms

Mark Watson

McGraw-Hill, Inc.

New York San Francisco Washington, D.C. Auckland Bogotá
Caracas Lisbon London Madrid Mexico City Milan
Montreal New Delhi San Juan Singapore
Sydney Tokyo Toronto

Library of Congress Cataloging-in-Publication Data

Watson, Mark, 1951–
    C++ power paradigms : constraint programming, genetic algorithms,
neural networks, using genetic algorithms to train recurrent neural
networks / Mark Watson.
        p.   cm.
    Includes bibliographical references and index.
    ISBN 0-07-911786-4   ISBN 0-07-911787-2 (pbk.)
    1. Object-oriented programming (Computer science)   2. C++
(Computer program language)   I. Title.
QA76.64.W38   1994
005.13'3—dc20   94-14984
                                                                                   CIP

1 2 3 4 5 6 7 8 9 0   DOH/DOH   9 9 8 7 6 5 4

ISBN 0-07-911787-2

The sponsoring editor for this book was Jennifer Holt DiGiovanna.
The executive editor was Joanne Slike. David M. McCandless was the
managing editor, Marc Damashek was the manuscript editor, the
director of production was Katherine G. Brown. This book was set in
ITC Century Light. It was composed in Blue Ridge Summit, Pa.

Printed and bound by Donnelley and Sons.

In order to receive additional information on these or any other
McGraw-Hill titles, in the United States please call 1-800-822-8158.   9117872
In other countries, contact your local McGraw-Hill representative.   MH94

Contents

Acknowledgments

I would like to thank my wife Carol for her encouragement while writing this book. I would like to thank Gady Costeff, Tim Kraft, Michael Romero, Pam Surko, and Carol Watson for reviewing this book.

I would like to thank Mark V Systems for the use of their ObjectMaker CAD system in creating the C++ class diagrams used in this book, and the developers at Borland International and at Apple Computer for writing the C++ development systems that I used to write the software contained in this book. I would like to thank Symantec for providing me with C++ compilers for both the Macintosh and Windows so that I could ensure the compatibility of the program examples with their environments. I would like to thank my parents Ken and Elaine for the use of their laser printer in preparing this book.

I would like to thank my agents Matt Wagner and Bill Gladstone at Waterside productions. I would like to thank Jennifer Holt DiGiovanna, my McGraw-Hill acquisitions editor, executive editor Joanne Slike, supervising editor David McCandless, manuscript editor Marc Damashek, and network supervisor Stephen Moore for their work on my manuscript.

I would like to thank my bosses at SAIC for providing a great technical environment: John Thompson and John Benepe. I would also like to thank my colleagues: Gregg Hanna, George Paprotny, Will Scarvie, Betty Torano, and Steve Vedder.

Introduction

I have three goals in writing this book. The first two are to provide good examples of the application of object-oriented analysis and design, and to provide a set of useful and reusable C++ classes that can drastically shorten development time of nontrivial programs.

My third goal in writing this book is more personal. I believe that the way we usually educate ourselves is wrong. I think that we learn best when we are having fun and can learn at our own pace those things that most interest us (in other words, when we are motivated!). Learning is a personal experience; we may collect facts and share experiences in a group, but real learning is a reflective experience in which we use quiet time to reorganize our thoughts and build our own frameworks for understanding the world around us. Most of our actions and thoughts occur fairly automatically and are based on previous experience. We cannot leave our minds in this "auto pilot" mode and expect to learn. I hope that this book will provide sufficient, enjoyable material for you to be excited about object-oriented software development using C++. I would rather my readers choose a single topic in this book, and really explore it via the software that I provide, than simply read the entire book through and not experiment with the software. Each of the four parts of this book is self-contained. Please read the book chapters in any order that interests you. You might enjoy, for example, starting with the chapters that provide sample applications before reading about the analysis, design, and implementation of the underlying C++ class libraries.

The Design and Development Process

The use of C++ has increased dramatically in the last few years. Many programming jobs now require C++ programming skills. Many new software development projects use C++ as the development language.

There are many C++ books. Most teach the syntax of the language, with few meaningful examples. Object-oriented programming with C++ is really more than simply learning a new programming notation or language. Object-oriented development is best learned by exposure to the process of designing and implementing good object-oriented libraries.

Object-oriented software development mixes the activities of analysis, design, and implementation in an iterative process. In developing real systems, initial design and prototyping always makes us reevaluate our analysis and preliminary design. In writing a book, it is difficult to convey a feel for this proper, iterative development process, since what you see in the book is the end product of a process that includes incremental analysis, design, and prototyping. Since I present the development of the C++ classes in the strict order of analysis, design, and implementation, I feel that it is important to remind my readers frequently that the proper way to develop software is by iterative analysis, design, and implementation. To this end, I discuss my prototype implementations and the design-improvement process.

Software is a resource. The value of that resource depends both on the immediate use of the software and on repeated future use. This book provides C++ class libraries for constraint-based programming, genetic algorithms, and neural networks. These classes permit designers and software developers to program "in the large"—that is, to concentrate on the overall design and global implementation details when building large systems. The use of these C++ class libraries will save development time and result in more powerful systems.

The Paradigms

Constraint programming supports a declarative style of programming that is useful for applications like graphics layout, computer-aided design, and the solution of routing problems. Constraint programs are useful in automating simple tasks that could be solved procedurally—it is often more convenient to declare the constraints of a system than to write custom procedural code to perform the same function. Internally, the C++ constraint classes use numerical methods like local propagation from graph theory and numerical relaxation. Users of the C++ constraint class can use the constraint system as a "black box," that is, without understanding the mathematical underpinnings used in the constraint satisfaction calculations. After implementing the C++ constraint classes, I develop two complete applications by subclassing the constraint classes for complex data types: placing furniture in a room subject to constraints and capital investment planning for small businesses.

Genetic algorithms are used for search and optimization. Genetic algorithms borrow the concepts of reproduction, mutation, and crossover from biology to efficiently solve some classes of problems that can be specified as a set of input parameters and a known fitness function. The fitness function provides a numerical value for the relative "fitness" for survival of each chromosome in a genetic population. Genetic algorithms provide a method for (sometimes) efficiently calculating a good (although perhaps not best) solution for complex search problems. After fully implementing the C++ genetic algorithm classes, I develop a complete application that optimizes the locations for a chain of hypothetical fast-food restaurants in a city, given building costs, a road network, population density, and competitive restaurant density data. This program calculates the number of restaurants to build and provides optimized locations.

Neural networks are often useful in building classification and control systems. Neural networks can be trained to recognize input patterns based on an internal state learned from previously classified input patterns. Similarly, neural networks are sometimes useful in control systems; network inputs are sensor readings, and network outputs are control signals for servos, temperature controls, etc. After implementing the C++ neural network classes, I develop two complete applications: a classifier for making buy/no buy decisions for home consumer goods and a neural network controller for a simple hypothetical factory.

Applications that require processing of continuously changing data require neural networks that contain feedback loops (recurrent neural networks). I develop C++ classes that use genetic algorithms to train recurrent neural networks. These C++ classes are used to search for a recurrent network that programs an artificial ant to move efficiently through its environment.

The three "Power Paradigms" presented in this book have something in common: none of them guarantees a solution to all problems. Rather, they are powerful techniques that can be applied to difficult problems. Hybrid systems are used when several different techniques must be applied to solve a problem at execution time. The following diagram demonstrates this architecture:

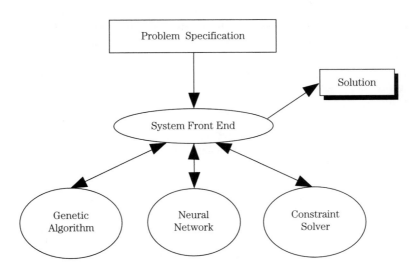

C++ Source Code Considerations

I assume that you already know how to program in C++. However, I do take the liberty of occasionally stepping back from the material in this book to reinforce some elementary C++ programming considerations. I always block off this additional text in a screened box, so that experienced C++ programmers can ignore it. For example:

Example text to cover elementary C++ programming techniques

Review material appears inside a screened box like this and can be ignored by experienced C++ programmers.

I have written the example C++ classes and demonstration programs to be as "bullet-proof" as possible, using runtime range checks when accessing data structures. Most of the example software will run faster if compiled with the FAST symbol defined, which turns off run-time safety checks. I also prefer to leave debug printout in my programs, but surround the printout statements with conditional compilation switches. For example:

```
#ifdef DEBUG
    cerr << "...propagating constraints:\n";
#endif

#ifndef FAST
    if (index > MAX_INDEX)       {
        cerr << "Error condition...\n";
    }
#endif
```

Notice that diagnostics sent to the error output stream are always printed, regardless of the state of the DEBUG compilation flag. I recommend that you enable the debug output when you first use the class libraries and example programs.

In writing the examples for this book, I frequently allocate data structures of fixed size (the size being dependent on a constant definition), rather than using dynamic allocation and reallocation. I have made this decision in order to make the example programs shorter and (I hope) easier to understand.*

I use Booch class diagrams (Booch 1991) to express the relationship of classes in the class libraries for constraint programming, genetic algorithms, and neural networks. This notation is shown in the following illustrations.

The following symbol is used to represent a C++ class:

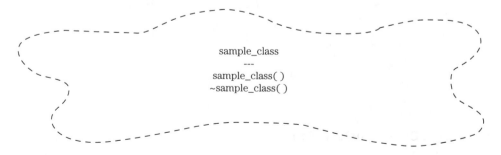

---

*To allow allocation of large data structures on the Windows heap, Windows programmers should define the conditional compilation flag WINDOWS when compiling the example programs and class libraries. Programmers using UNIX, Macintosh, NT, and OS/2 should not define the compilation flag WINDOWS.

The first line of text inside the class symbol is the name of the class. After a separator line ("---"), I list the public interface to the class.

The following example shows a base class and a derived class:

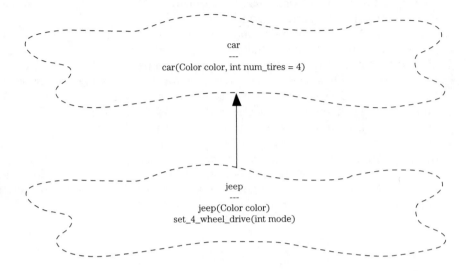

In this diagram, the class `jeep` is derived from the class `car`, and defines specialized behavior (the ability to turn four-wheel drive off and on).

Often classes use other classes by containing instances of these other classes. For example, an instance of the class `car` will contain one or more `tire` objects:

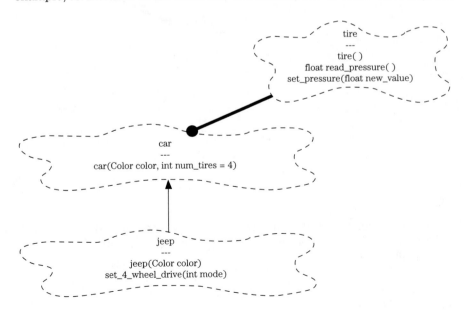

This diagram shows two types of relationships between classes (or the instances of classes): is-a and has-a relationships. The class `jeep` is derived from class `car` (i.e., `jeep` is a subclass of class `car`); a `jeep` is a type of `car` (is-a car). A `car` (or `jeep`) contains `tire` objects (has-a relationship). Note that a `jeep` contains `tires` because its superclass `car` contains `tires`.

Note that I do not always include all public member functions in the class diagrams; for example, I assume that every C++ class will have a destructor, so I often choose not to show destructors in the class diagrams. When I use a C++ class library, I prefer to use a class diagram as a reference for the commonly used public member functions. The class diagram serves as a memory-enhancing artifact both for these public member functions and for the relationship between classes.

It is sometimes useful to have utility classes that can be used to implement other classes. For example, some of the classes developed in this book use a random-number generation object, so I treat the class `RandomSequence` as a utility class. Assuming that our `car` and `jeep` C++ objects have a simulation behavior, it might be useful to use a random-number generating object that is an instance of a class utility `RandomSequence`:

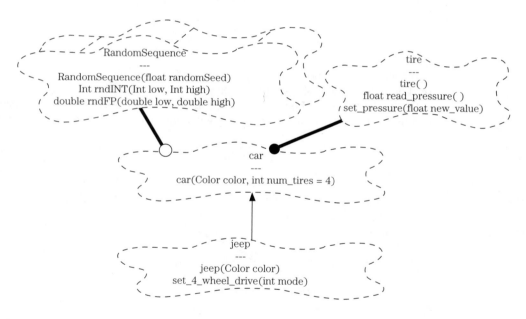

Source Listings

I modified my usual formatting style in order to make the program listings more readable. Although I normally prefer placing opening curly brackets at the end of a line like this:

```
if (buffer_count >= BUFFER_SIZE) {
    flush_buffer();
```

```
        buffer_count = 0;
    }
```

in this book I match up opening and closing curly brackets like this:

```
if (buffer_count >= BUFFER_SIZE)
{   flush_buffer();
    buffer_count = 0;
}
```

Because of the limitation on the number of columns in a book, I frequently resort to indenting source code only two spaces per indentation level, rather than my usual preference of four spaces.

Reuse of Software

Please feel free to reuse the software contained in this book in compiled form. With the exception of the VariGenSearch™ genetic search algorithm and software developed in Chapter 12, I release all commercial rights to the software in this book when it is in compiled form and contained in any programs that you write. You may not distribute the software contained in this book in source code form without written permission from the author. This software is provided on an "as is" basis; neither the author nor McGraw-Hill makes any warranties regarding the fitness or correctness of the software in this book.

The VariGenSearch™ algorithm and software can be used in any noncommercial application. Please write for permission and licensing to use VariGenSearch™ in commercial applications.

Source Code Availability

In addition to the disk purchased with this book, you can order the software from my book *Portable GUI Development with C++* (McGraw-Hill, 1993), for portable development on the Windows, Macintosh, and X Windows platforms, for $12 on a disk. The C++ source code in this book and on the software disk may not be redistributed. I reserve the right to supply updated versions of the software on disk, containing recent bug-fixes and enhancements. When I send out disks, I enclose the current (often enhanced) versions, so the software on the disk will not in general match exactly what is in this book (in other words, I reserve the right to send you bug-fixes and improvements).Contact me at

Mark Watson
535 Mar Vista Dr.
Solana Beach, CA 92075

My CompuServe account is 75765,556 and my BIX e-mail address is wmark. I can be reached as mwa@netcom.com on the Internet. I welcome correspondence, preferably via e-mail. If you prefer, I can e-mail you via the Internet a uuencoded, compressed UNIX tar file for $8 (software in this book) or $12 (software for both this book and my portable GUI book).

My company, Mark Watson Associates, has several interesting software products for Artificial Intelligence, optimization, and GUI development. Future products will include virtual reality toolkits. You can send me e-mail requesting more information.

Constraint Programming

Analysis for the Constraint Programming Classes

Most computer program modules are executed in some predetermined sequence. Programmers may view their program modules as a linear sequence of executable steps, and perhaps also consider preconceived alternate paths taken in the flow of execution. Constraint programming uses known constraints (or relationships) among objects being modeled in programs to solve application problems without custom programming.

This chapter deals with the analysis for constraint C++ classes. In the object-oriented software development methodology, I start analyzing a problem by decomposing it into its fundamental elements. During the analysis, I refine my understanding of the problem, laying all of the pieces out for a clear view. In the next chapter, we take these ideas for doing constraint programming and create class hierarchies to hide the programming details.

The goal in producing constraint satisfaction C++ classes is to add the utility of constraint-based programming to the object model of software development. Constraint objects model the relationships among data objects, and provide a formalism (sometimes) to solve application problems by declaring the relationships or constraints among objects, rather than by explicitly programming a series of computational steps.

Constraint programming is a new way to think about constructing software. As with all new techniques, constraint programming is not a "silver bullet" that magically solves programming problems. Rather, constraint programming is an alternative notation for specifying application problems.

1.1 Definition of Terms

A *constraint object* has a value, which can be a complex data structure, and is subject to zero or more constraints. A constraint can be any relationship among different constraint objects.

A *constraint propagation network* is a graph data structure that contains both constraint objects and constraints. We will represent both constraint objects and constraints as C++ data objects. The arcs, or links, in a propagation network will be represented by pointers to both constraint objects and constraints. Local propagation can be used to propagate constraints in a propagation network if the conditions discussed in Sec. 1.2 are met.

Relaxation is the search for constraint values that minimize the error for a constraint network.

1.2   A Simple Example Introduces the Concepts of Constraint Programming

Both Leler (1988) and Abelson/Sussman (1985) use the example of temperature conversion between centigrade and Fahrenheit to introduce constraint programming. I will also use this example, but cast it in terms of interacting objects.

Constraints are viewed as objects connected to other data objects called "constraint" data objects. Furthermore, these constraint data objects come in two types (classes): constant and variable. Variable-type data objects must have an external behavior for setting their state.

This class hierarchy can be further extended for different types of variable and constant objects. For example, you may want numerical data types in "constraint" objects, or structured data types representing objects like rectangles, circles, etc.

Figure 1.1 shows a constraint propagation graph for the temperature conversion example that solves the equation

```
1.8*C + 32 = F
```

There are addition and multiplication constraint objects in Figure 1.1. The behavior of the addition constraint object can be expressed by

```
A + B = C
```

Using this formula, if the values of two of the three variables A, B, and C are known, the value of the third can be calculated by the + constraint object. The + constraint object constrains its output to be equal to the sum of its inputs. A similar relationship holds for the inputs and output of the multiplication constraint object.

The constraint propagation network in Figure 1.1 can be efficiently solved, given a value for either "variable" constraint object, using a technique known as "local propagation" (Leler (1988) and Abelson/Sussman (1985)). The C++ classes to be designed and implemented in Chapter 2 will have no difficulty solving simple problems like the one represented in Figure 1.1. A more difficult problem is shown in Figure 1.2, where the network represents the problem

```
A * A = B
```

Even though this equation is simpler than the temperature conversion relationship, it cannot be directly solved using simple local propagation techniques because

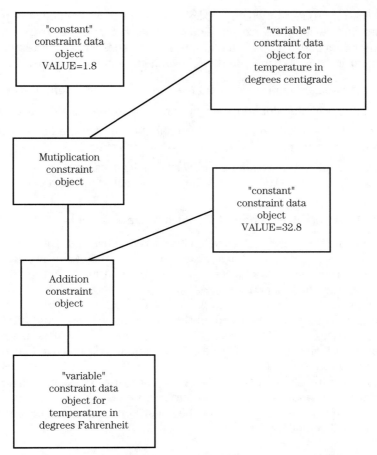

Figure 1.1 Constraint propagation network used to solve temperature conversion problems.

the * constraint object's inputs share a common data constraint. That is, the * constraint has a cycle because both inputs depend on A. What is the desired behavior of C++ constraint classes when constraint objects are created that contain cycles?

For constraint propagation graphs that contain one or more cycles, you can use the numerical relaxation technique. As you will see in Chapter 2, numerical relax-

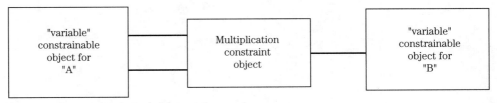

Figure 1.2 Propagation network that contains a cycle.

ation is a search process in which multiple random values are assigned to variable constraints, and these values are modified to reduce the sum of the errors calculated by the constraints in the propagation graph. These issues will be addressed in Chapter 2; for now, it suffices to include the following ideas in our analysis:

1. Constraint satisfaction problems can be expressed as constraint graphs.
2. Constraint graphs that contain no cycles are easy to solve with local propagation.
3. If you cannot use local propagation, you should then try the numerical analysis technique of relaxation.
4. There are problems that cannot be (easily) solved using these constraint programming techniques. This failure will not be detected until execution time.

1.3 Extensibility for Defining New Types of Constraint Data Objects

The simple example in Sec. 1.1 used unstructured constraint data objects whose "value" could be expressed as a single floating-point number. Many application problems require structured data objects. For example, you may want your constraint data objects to take on geometric shapes.

For example, in Chapter 3 I use the constraint C++ classes to write an application that places furniture in a room based on the constraints of room and furniture size. Data objects must be able to represent, in two dimensions, shapes like rectangles and circles. Constraint objects must be able to contain and manage constraint data objects of many different types.

In Chapter 4, I use the constraint C++ classes to write a program that optimizes capital equipment purchases subject to constraints.

You will see in Chapters 3 and 4 that the constraint classes can be subclassed to support arbitrarily complex data types.

2

Design and Implementation of the C++ Constraint Programming Classes

I indicated application-domain problems that constraint objects can solve in Chapter 1. I also hinted that in some cases the internal behavior of constraint objects is very complex: constraint objects must be able to detect a situation in which they are part of a cycle in a constraint propagation graph, and use numerical relaxation techniques. Constraint objects in a network are allowed to alter the states of other constraint objects. We are not, strictly speaking, violating the principle of encapsulation here since we can think of the constraint propagation graph as being distributed private data created and shared by a framework or mechanism built from a set of constraint objects. Clients of a framework of constraint objects do not have access to this distributed private data. The external interface to a framework of constraint objects should always be simple, effectively hiding the internal complex behavior of local propagation and numerical relaxation.

Many constraint problems will only be solvable using relaxation techniques, but relaxation should be the method of last resort—always try local propagation first.

The analysis in Chapter 1 dealt with the problem of constraint programming. In this chapter, we create class hierarchies that hide the implementation details discovered in Chapter 1.

2.1 Managing the Interactions of Constraint Objects

The most interesting aspect of constraint class design will be the management of constraint objects. The basic problem is to know how many constraint objects have been created, and to be able to iterate over them. There are two good ways to control the global behavior of the individual constraint objects in a system: through static class behavior and container classes.

2.1.1 Using static class behavior to manage constraint objects

C++ static class member data attributes and functions can be used to keep track of and control all instances of a class. Static data attributes are allocated once for an entire C++ class and are shared by all instances of a class. They are effectively "global data" to all instances of a class, while being hidden from all other objects in the system if declared private.

**Using static class variables to maintain
a count of the number of instances of a class**

```
class count_instances
{
 public:
    count_instances()
    {
        count++; // increment count in constructor
    }
    ~count_instances()
    {
        count--; // decrement count in the destructor
    }
    static int number_of_instances()
    {
        return count;
    }
 private:
    static int count;
};

// the linker complains if we do not allocate storage for
// static class variables:
int count_instances::count = 0;
  main()
{
    count_instances  c1, c2; // call the constructor twice
    cout << "There are " << count_instances::number_of_instances()
        << " count_instances objects\n";
}

// Note: if the static member data attribute "count" were public,
// then the following would be legal:

    int num_objects=count_instances::count; // illegal private access
```

When I developed the prototype for the C++ constraint library, I used static member functions and data to keep track of all types of constraint objects that had been constructed, and to solve constraint problems.

The disadvantage of this method is that it keeps track of all constraint objects in the program as one set; there are applications in which it is useful to have more than a single set of cooperating constraint objects.

2.1.2 Using separate constraint object collection classes

Collection objects are useful for managing sets of data objects. A physical analogy is helpful: if you keep several marbles in a bag, the marbles are data objects, and the bag is a collection object. We usually define the following standard behaviors for collection classes:

- Add data objects to a collection
- Remove data objects from a collection
- Ask the collection how many data objects it contains
- Access a specific object in the collection

The behavior for accessing specific objects in the collection is implemented by defining a C++ operator [] function. Typically, this is a minimum behavior for a collection class, additional behaviors being associated with the types of objects that can be stored in a collection.

Here, we will design and implement the C++ class constraint_collection, which will provide the "standard" collection behavior for constraint objects. Instances of this class will also provide the complex behavior of constraint satisfaction using local propagation and numerical relaxation. By allowing multiple instances of the constraint_collection class, you can use multiple concurrent constraint systems in your programs.

2.2 Constraint Class Structure

Figure 2.1 shows an object interaction diagram for data and constraint objects, using the notation of Booch (1991).

2.3 C++ Interface for the Constraint Classes

In this section, I list the C++ header (include) files for the classes shown in Figure 2.1 and for the random number utility class (found in the util directory on the software disk).

The following listing shows the C++ interface for the class RandomSequence, which is used for the constraint, genetic algorithm, and neural network classes in this book (located in the util directory on the software disk):

```
// File: randseq.h
//
// Description: This file contains the C++ interface to class
//              RandomSequence.  This is a utility class used
//              by the constraint, genetic algorithm, and
//              neural network classes.
//
// By Mark Watson.  This code is placed in the public domain.
//

#ifndef randseq_h
#define randseq_h
class RandomSequence
{
  public:
```

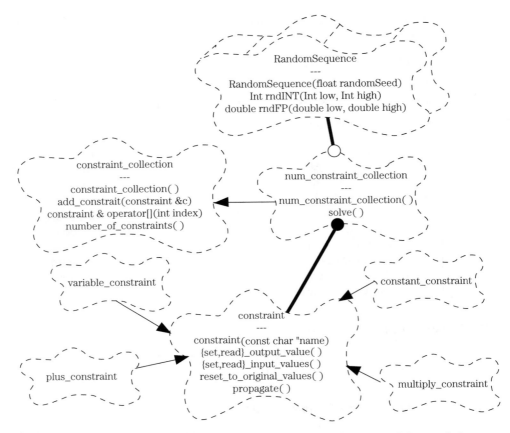

Figure 2.1 Classes `variable_constraint` and `constant_constraint` are subclasses of class con straint. Class `constraint_collection` contains and controls multiple constraint objects.

```
    RandomSequence(float randomSeed = 10.0);
    int    rndINT(int low, int high);
    double rndFP(double low, double high);

  private:
    void    next_random_sequence();
    double rand_util();
    float   randomseed;
    int     random_counter;
    int     rndcalcflag;
    double oldrand[55];
};

#endif
```

The `RandomSequence` class is used to provide more control over the random numbers used to solve constraint, genetic algorithm, and neural network C++ classes in this book. By setting compilation flags for the implementation file `ranseq.cp`, you can use default library routines or generate your own repeatable pseudorandom number sequences. The constructor `RandomSequence` takes an optional argument, which is a seed value for generating random number sequences. You can regenerate the same sequence by using the same seed value. The member functions `rndINT` and `rndFP` return a pseudorandom number in a specified range as either an `int` or a `float`.

The following listing shows the C++ interface for the class constraint.

```
// File: constrn.h
//
// Description: This file contains the C++ interface for the class
//              constraint.  This class is an abstract base class
//              (the virtual member function propagate() is set to zero),
//              so you cannot create instances of this class.  Our
//              constraint class library will contain 5 subclasses of
//              this class: variable_constraint, constant_constraint,
//              plus_constraint, multiply_constraint, and
//              geometric_constraint.  You will probably create more
//              derived constraint classes in your applications.
//
//
// This software may be used without restriction in compiled form. This
// source code cannot be redistributed without permission.
//
#ifndef constrn_h
#define constrn_h

#include "randseq.h"

#include <iostream.h>
#include <math.h>
#include <stdlib.h>

const int FALSE = 0;
const int TRUE = 1;

const int NO_TYPE = 0;

const int MAX_NODES = 10;
const int MAX_GRID = 256;
const int NAME_LEN = 16;

// We need to define a forward reference for constraint_collection.
// This is used in constraint::set_my_container(), which records
// the container that holds a constraint object.

class constraint_collection;

class constraint   // abstract base class
{
 public:
  constraint(const char *my_name);

  inline void set_in_node(int index, constraint &a_node)
  {
    if (index >= 0 && index < MAX_NODES) {
      in_nodes[index] = &a_node;
      num_in_nodes++;
    }
  }

  inline void set_out_node(int index, constraint &a_node)
```

```
    {
      if (index >= 0 && index < MAX_NODES) {
        out_nodes[index] = &a_node;
        num_out_nodes++;
      }
    }
    void set_output_value(float new_value) { value = new_value; }
    float read_output_value() { return value; }
    void set_input_value(int index, float new_value)
    {
      if (index >= 0 && index < MAX_NODES) {
        in_nodes[index]->set_output_value(new_value);
      }
    }

    virtual int my_type()
    {
      return NO_TYPE;
    }

    // Note: the following is a const char *, so it can only be set in
    //        the constructor (see constrn.cp):
    const char *name;

    virtual float propagate() = 0;   // make this an abstract base class

    void save_original_value()
    {
      original_value = value;
    }

    void reset_to_original_value()
    {
      value = original_value;
    }

    float read_original_value()
    {
      return original_value;
    }

    void set_my_container(constraint_collection *container)
    {
      my_container = container;
    }

    constraint_collection * container()
    {
      return my_container;
    }

  protected:
    constraint *in_nodes[MAX_NODES];
    constraint *out_nodes[MAX_NODES];
    constraint_collection *my_container;
    int num_in_nodes;
    int num_out_nodes;
    float value;
    float original_value;
    int check_cycle_flag;   // temporary storage for graph sweeps
    int has_a_cycle_flag;
};

#endif
```

The class `constraint` is the base class used for deriving all other constraint object classes in this book. The constructor for a constraint object takes a single `const char *` argument, which is a name for the object; this name is useful for identifying objects in diagnostic printouts. The constraint object name is not used internally in the constraint classes.

Constraint objects are usually interconnected by directed links. The output of one object can be the input to another. When constraint objects are contained in graph data structures, we often call them nodes. The member function `set_out_node` connects another constraint object to the output of this constraint object. The member function `set_output_value` is used to overwrite the current numerical value of this constraint object.

Encapsulation of member data

Note in this listing that I have made the following declaration public:

```
const char *name;
```

Usually, I make member data private (or protected when I want to allow member functions of derived classes access to the data) for encapsulation, or data hiding. Here I show a different approach that you will also find useful in designing your classes.

```
class demo
{
 public:
    demo(const char * name_value = "default_name");
    const char * name;
};

demo::demo(const char * name_value)   :   name(name_value)
{
}
```

The constructor sets the value of the `const char *` member data name. As long as you only call C++ and ANSI C functions (with C prototypes), your programs will not be able to change the value of `name`, which is what we want in this case.

I show the following as an alternative. Usually, I prefer to use member access functions to control access to private or protected data. For example:

```
class demo
{
 public:
    demo(const char * name_value = "default_name");
    const char *get_name();
    // Note: Do not declare 'set_name()' since you do not want to
    //       allow a program to change an object's name once it is set.
 private:
    char * name;
};
```

```
demo::demo(const char * name_value)  :  name(name_value)
{
}

const char * demo::get_name()
{
    return name;
}
```

The following listing shows the C++ interface for the class `constant_constraint`.

```
// File: constant.h
//
// Description: This file contains the C++ interface for the class
//              constant_constraint.  It is derived from the class
//              constraint, with the behavior that its value (a floating-point
//              number) cannot be changed during constraint
//              network relaxation.
//
//
// This software may be used without restriction in compiled form. This
// source code may not be redistributed without permission.
//
#ifndef __constant
#define __constant

#include "constrn.h"

#include <iostream.h>
#include <math.h>

const int CONSTANT_TYPE = 21;

class constraint_collection;

class constant_constraint : public constraint
{
 public:
  constant_constraint(const char *my_name = "no_name");
  inline float set_value(float new_value) { value = new_value;
      return value; }
  inline float read_value() { return value; }
  inline virtual float return_error() { return original_value -
      value; }
  float propagate();

  virtual int my_type() { return CONSTANT_TYPE; }
  char name[NAME_LEN];
  void save_original_value();
  void reset_to_original_value();
  float read_original_value() { return original_value; }
  void set_my_container(constraint_collection *container)
  {
    my_container = container;
  }

 protected:

};

#endif
```

The following listing shows the C++ interface for the class `variable_constraint`:

```
// File: variable.h
//
// Description: This file contains the C++ interface for the class
//              variable_constraint, and is derived from the class constraint.
//
//
// This software may be used without restriction in compiled form. This
// source code may not be redistributed without permission.
//
#ifndef __variable
#define __variable

#include "constrn.h"

#include <iostream.h>

#include <math.h>

const int VARIABLE_TYPE = 49;

class constraint_collection;

class variable_constraint : public constraint
{
 public:
   variable_constraint(const char *my_name = "no_name");
   inline float set_value(float new_value) { value = new_value;
       return value; }
   inline float read_value() { return value; }
   inline virtual float return_error() { return original_value -
       value; }
   float propagate();

   virtual int my_type() { return VARIABLE_TYPE; }

   char name[NAME_LEN];
   void save_original_value();
   void reset_to_original_value();
   float read_original_value() { return original_value; }

   void set_my_container(constraint_collection *container)
   {
     my_container = container;
   }
 protected:

};

#endif
```

The following listing shows the C++ interface for the class `multiply_constraint`.

```
// File: multiply.h
//
// Description: This file contains the C++ interface for the class
```

```
//             multiply_constraint, and is derived from the class constraint.
//             This class constrains the value of the constraint object
//             connected to its output connection to be the product of the
//             values of the connection objects connected to its input
//             connections.
//
//
// This software may be used without restriction in compiled form. This
// source code may not be redistributed without permission.
//
#ifndef __multiply
#define __multiply

#include "constrn.h"

#include <iostream.h>

#include <math.h>

const int MULTIPLY_TYPE = 210;

class constraint_collection;

class multiply_constraint : public constraint
{
 public:
  multiply_constraint(const char *my_name = "no_name");
  inline virtual float return_error() { return original_value -
         value; }
  float propagate();
  virtual int my_type() { return MULTIPLY_TYPE; }
 protected:

};

#endif
```

The following listing shows the C++ interface for the class `plus_constraint`.

```
// File: plus.h
//
// Description: This file contains the C++ interface for the class
//             plus_constraint, and is derived from the class constraint.
//             This class constrains the value of the constraint object
//             connected to its output connection to be the sum of the
//             values of the connection objects connected to its input
//             connections.
//
//
// This software may be used without restriction in compiled form. This
// source code may not be redistributed without permission.
//
#ifndef __plus
#define __plus

#include "constrn.h"

#include <iostream.h>

#include <math.h>

const int PLUS_TYPE = 98;
```

```
class constraint_collection;

class plus_constraint : public constraint
{
 public:
  plus_constraint(const char *my_name = "no_name");
  float propagate();
  virtual int my_type() { return PLUS_TYPE; }
 protected:

};

#endif
```

The following listing of file cnstrCol.h shows the C++ interface for the class constraint_collection.

```
// File: cnstrCol.h
//
// Description: The constraint_collection class acts as a normal collection,
//              and also provides the behavior of constraint satisfaction
//              networks.  An instance of the constraint_collection class can
//              solve the constraint problem represented by the contained
//              constraint nodes by simple propagation and by numerical
//              relaxation.
//
//
// This software may be used without restriction in compiled form. This
// source code may not be redistributed without permission.
//
#ifndef cnstrCol_h
#define cnstrCol_h

#include "constrn.h"

#ifdef WINDOWS
#include "windows.h"
#endif

const int MAX_IN_COLLECTION = MAX_NODES;

class constraint_collection
{
 public:
     constraint_collection();
    ~constraint_collection();
       virtual int solve() = 0;
     inline int read_relaxation_mode_flag()
     {
       return relaxation_mode_flag;
     }
     inline void set_relaxation_mode_flag(int new_value)
     { relaxation_mode_flag=new_value; }
     constraint & operator[](int index);
     void add_constraint(constraint &new_constraint)
     {
       if (num_constraints < (MAX_IN_COLLECTION - 1))
       {
           class_constraints[num_constraints++] = &new_constraint;
           new_constraint.set_my_container(this);
       }                 }
```

```
        const int get_num_constraints()
        {
          return num_constraints;
        }

    protected:
        int num_constraints;
        constraint * class_constraints[MAX_IN_COLLECTION];
        int num_relaxation_nodes;
        int relaxation_mode_flag;
        int relaxation_node_indices[MAX_NODES];
        float relaxation_error[MAX_GRID];
        int relaxation();
        RandomSequence *random_sequence;
};

#endif
```

When I prototyped the class `constraint_collection`, I implemented constraint propagation for numerical constraint objects, as seen in Figures 1.1 and 1.2. This was fine for a prototype, but when I started writing more constraint data classes, I decided to split the class `constraint_collection` into two classes:

- `constraint_collection` now contains member data for storing links to constraint objects stored in the collection

- `num_constraint_collection` is derived from `constraint_collection` and adds constraint-solving behavior for numerical constraint data objects

The following listing of file numcncol.h shows the C++ interface for the class `num_constraint_collection`.

```
// File: numcncol.h
//
// Description: This file contains the C++ interface for
//              class num_constraint_collection. This
//              class inherits from constraint_collection,
//              adding data and behavior for the solve methods.
//
//
// This software may be used without restriction in compiled form. This
// source code may not be redistributed without permission.
//
#ifndef numcncol_h
#define numcncol_h

#include "cnstrcol.h"

class num_constraint_collection : public constraint_collection
{
 public:
     num_constraint_collection();
    ~num_constraint_collection();
       virtual int solve();
     virtual int solve_by_relaxation(int depth);

 protected:
#ifndef WINDOWS
     float relaxation_values[MAX_NODES][MAX_GRID];
```

```
#else
     float FAR * relaxation_values[MAX_NODES];
     HANDLE r_handles[MAX_NODES];
#endif
     float v_min[MAX_NODES];
     float v_max[MAX_NODES];
};

#endif
```

The class num_constraint_collection is derived from the class constraint_collection and adds both protected member data for use in numerical relaxation and member functions for solving numerical constraint problems.

Compiling for Microsoft Windows

Note that if this file is compiled with the WINDOWS compile flag set, then the large blocks of data needed for the relaxation calculations are stored on the Windows heap. This is not necessary for Macintosh, UNIX, OS/2 and NT programs. Throughout this book, I allocate large blocks of storage on the Windows heap to allow large problems to be solved.

This class added behavior for dealing with numerical constraints. In Sec. 3.3, I will specify the interface for the two classes geometric_constraint and geometric_constraint_collection, which are derived from the classes defined in this chapter.

2.4 C++ Implementation of the Constraint Classes

In this section, we list the C++ source files for the classes shown in Figure 2.1.

The following listing of randseq.cp shows the implementation of the class utility RandomSequence.

```
// File: randseq.cp
//
// Description: This file contains the C++ implementation for the class
//              RandomSequence.  This is a utility class used by the
//              constraint, genetic algorithm, and neural network
//              classes.
//
//              For some problems, it is very useful to be able to generate
//              the same series of pseudorandom numbers.  Comment out
//              the definition of the constant USE_LIBRARY to cause
//              instances of class RandomSequence to produce identical
//              pseudorandom sequences when constructed with the same
//              argument.
//
//
// By Mark Watson.  This code is placed in the public domain.
//

#define USE_LIBRARY 1

#include "randseq.h"
#include <math.h>
```

```
#ifdef USE_LIBRARY
#include <stdlib.h>
#endif

static float initialSeed = 0.7123152;

//
//          Class constructor: RandomSequence
//
//          Note: the randomSeed value should be between 0.0 and 1.0
//
RandomSequence::RandomSequence(float randomSeed)
{
  // Tweak input argument (a little) to get it in range:
  if ( randomSeed < 0.0) randomSeed = - randomSeed;
  if ( randomSeed > 0.999)  randomSeed *= 0.1;
  if ( randomSeed > 0.999)  randomSeed *= 0.1;

  // Override argument if the value was too far out of range:
  if (randomSeed >  0.999 || randomSeed < 0.01)
  {
     initialSeed *= 0.9842134;
     randomSeed = initialSeed;
     if (initialSeed < 0.1)  initialSeed *= 0.99991;
  }

#ifdef USE_LIBRARY
  randomize();
  float rr = rand();
  rr = rr / 70000.0;
  initialSeed = rr;
#endif

  int ran_index, ii;
  double new_random, prev_random;

  oldrand[54] = randomSeed;
  for (int k=0; k<54; k++)  oldrand[k] = 0.1 + (float)k * 0.016;
  new_random = 0.000000001;
  prev_random = randomSeed;
  for(ran_index = 1 ; ran_index <= 540; ran_index++)
  {
    ii = (21*ran_index)%54;
    oldrand[ii] = new_random;
    new_random = prev_random-new_random;
    if(new_random<0.0) new_random = new_random + 1.0;
    prev_random = oldrand[ii];
  }

  next_random_sequence();
  next_random_sequence();
  next_random_sequence();
  next_random_sequence();

  random_counter = 0;
  }

void RandomSequence::next_random_sequence()
/* Create next batch of 55 random numbers */
{
    int ran_index;
    double new_random;
    for(ran_index = 0; ran_index < 24; ran_index++)
    {
        new_random = oldrand[ran_index] - oldrand[ran_index+31];
        if(new_random <}< 0.0) new_random = new_random + 1.0;
```

```
            oldrand[ran_index] = new_random;
        }
    for(ran_index = 24; ran_index < 55; ran_index++)
        {
            new_random = oldrand [ran_index] - oldrand [ran_index-24];
            if(new_random <0.0) new_random = new_random + 1.0;
            oldrand[ran_index] = new_random;
        }
}

int RandomSequence::rndINT(int low, int high)
{
    int ret_val;
    if(low >= high) {
        ret_val = low;
    } else {
        ret_val = (int)((rand_util() * (high - low + 1)) + low;
        if(ret_val > high) ret_val = high;
    }
    return(ret_val);
}

double RandomSequence::rndFP(double low, double high)
{
    return (rand_util() * (high - low)) + low;
}

double RandomSequence::rand_util() // Knuth subtractive method
{
#ifndef USE_LIBRARY
    random_counter++;
    if(random_counter >= 55)
    {
        random_counter = 1;
        next_random_sequence();
    }
    return  oldrand[random_counter];
#else
    return ((float)(random(10000))) * 0.0001;
#endif

}
```

Random numbers

Generating random number sequences is an important part of solving many problems. All three class libraries developed in this book rely on the Random Sequence class.

For many problems, we want new sequences of random numbers generated every time the program is executed. For other applications, it is important to be able to regenerate the same sequences of random numbers so that program results can be exactly duplicated. If the compiler flag USE_LIBRARY is set, then instances of this class use the C++ library random functions to initialize the data for generating random numbers; this has the effect of creating new, irreproducible sequences of random numbers. If this compiler flag is not set, then an instance of the class RandomSequence will generate the same sequence of random numbers that another RandomSequence object would if the random seed argument to the constructor has the same value.

The following listing shows the implementation of the abstract base class `constraint`.

```
// File: constrn.cp
//
// Description: This file contains the C++ interface for the
//              class constraint
//
//
// This software may be used without restriction in compiled form. This
// source code may not be redistributed without permission.
//
#include "constrn.h"
#include "string.h"

//
//          Class constructor: constraint
//

constraint::constraint(const char *my_name) : name(my_name)
{
#ifdef DEBUG
  cerr << "entering base class 'constraint' constructor: "
       << my_name << "\n";
#endif

}
```

The following listing of constant.cp shows the implementation of the class `constant_constraint`.

```
// File: constant.cp
//
// Description: This file contains the C++ implementation of the class
//              constant_constraint
//
//
// This software may be used without restriction in compiled form. This
// source code may not be redistributed without permission.
//
#include "constant.h"
#include <string.h>

//
//          Class constructor: constant_constraint
//
constant_constraint::constant_constraint(const char *my_name)
           : constraint(name)
{
#ifdef DEBUG
  cerr << "entering derived class 'constant_constraint' constructor: "
       << my_name << "\n";
#endif
}

//
//          The propagate function for constant nodes
//          does nothing
//
```

```
float constant_constraint::propagate()
{
  // constant and constant constraints do not propagate values
  return 0;
}
```

The following listing of variable.cp shows the implementation of the class variable_constraint.

```
// File: variable.cp
//
// Description: This file tests my first ideas on doing constraint-
//              based programming using constraint propagation graphs.
//
//
// This software may be used without restriction in compiled form.
// This source code may not be redistributed without permission.
//
#include "variable.h"
#include "cnstrCol.h"

//
//          Class constraint: variable_constraint
//

variable_constraint::variable_constraint(const char *my_name)
           : constraint(my_name)
{
    cerr << "entering derived class 'variable_constraint' constructor: "
         << my_name << "\n";
}

float variable_constraint::propagate()
{
    // variable and constant constraints do not propagate values
    return 0;
}
```

The following listing shows the implementation of class multiply_constraint.

```
// File: multiply.cp
//
// Description: This file contains the implementation of the C++
//              multiply_constraint class
//
//
// This software may be used without restriction in compiled form. This
// source code may not be redistributed without permission.
//
#include "multiply.h"
#include "cnstrCol.h"

//
//          Class constructor: multiply_constraint
//

multiply_constraint::multiply_constraint(const char *my_name)
         : constraint(my_name)
{
#ifdef DEBUG
```

```
        cerr << "entering derived class 'multiply_constraint' constructor: "
            <<my_name << "\n";
#endif
}
//
//          Member function propagate for the class
//          multiply_constraint returns the error
//          in calculating output = input1 * input2,
//          where two out of three of these variables
//          are known.
//

float multiply_constraint::propagate()
{
  if (my_container == NULL)
  {
      cerr << "NULL my_container pointer in"
          << " multiply_constraint::propagate\n";
      exit(1);
  }
  if (my_container->read_relaxation_mode_flag() == 0)
  {
      // Here, we are in LOCAL PROPAGATION mode, so we
      // simply calculate one of the values for (input1, input2,
      // or output) if the other two are known:

      if ((in_nodes[0]->read_output_value() != -9999) &&
          (in_nodes[1]->read_output_value() != -9999))
      {

        float new_output = in_nodes[0]->read_output_value()
                    * in_nodes[1]->read_output_value();
#ifdef DEBUG
        cerr << "multiply_constraint::propagate: node: "
            << name << " setting output to "
            << new_output << "\n";
#endif
        out_nodes[0]->set_output_value(new_output);
        value = new_output;
      }
      if ((in_nodes[0]->read_output_value() == -9999) &&
          (in_nodes[1]->read_output_value() != -9999) &&
          (value != -9999))
      {
        float new_input = value / in_nodes[1]->read_output_value();
#ifdef DEBUG
        cerr << "multiply_constraint::propagate: node: "
            << name << " setting input 0 to "
            << new_input << "\n";
#endif
        in_nodes[0]->set_output_value(new_input);
      }
      if ((in_nodes[1]->read_output_value() == -9999) &&
          (in_nodes[0]->read_output_value() != -9999) &&
          (value != -9999))
      {
        float new_input = value / in_nodes[0]->read_output_value();
#ifdef DEBUG
        cerr << "multiply_constraint::propagate: node: "
            << name << " setting input 1 to "
            << new_input << "\n";
#endif
        in_nodes[1]->set_output_value(new_input);
      }
```

```
            return return_error();

    } else
        //
        // Here, we are in relaxation mode, so just calculate error.
        // The class constraint_collection member functions solve
        // and solve_by_relaxation use the error that is calculated
        // here to reduce the amount of error for all constraint
        // objects in the collection.
        //
        return (in_nodes[0]->read_output_value() *
                in_nodes[1]->read_output_value())
              - out_nodes[0]->read_original_value();
}
```

The following listing shows the implementation of class plus_constraint.

```
// File: plus.cp
//
// Description: This file contains the implementation of the class
//              plus_constraint
//
//
// This software may be used without restriction in compiled form. This
// source code may not be redistributed without permission.
//
#include "plus.h"
#include "cnstrCol.h"

//
//          Class constructor: plus_constraint
//

plus_constraint::plus_constraint(const char *my_name)
        : constraint(my_name)
{
#ifdef DEBUG
  cerr << "entering derived class 'plus_constraint' constructor: "
       << my_name << "\n";
#endif
}

//
//          Member function propagate for the class
//          plus_constraint returns the error
//          in calculating output = input1 + input2,
//          where two out of three of these variables
//          are known.
//
float plus_constraint::propagate()
{
  if (my_container == NULL) {
     cerr << "NULL my_container pointer in plus_constraint::"
          << "propagate\n";
     exit(1);
  }
  if (my_container->read_relaxation_mode_flag() == 0)
  {
     // Here, we are in LOCAL PROPAGATION mode, so we
     // simply calculate one of the values for (input1, input2,
     // or output) if the other two are known:
     if ((in_nodes[0]->read_output_value() != -9999) &&
```

```
                          (in_nodes[1]->read_output_value() != -9999))
                  {
                    float new_output = in_nodes[0]->read_output_value()
                             + in_nodes[1]->read_output_value();
#ifdef DEBUG
                    cerr << "plus_constraint::propagate: node: "
                          << name << " setting output to "
                          << new_output << "\n";
#endif
                    out_nodes[0]->set_output_value(new_output);
                    value = new_output;
                  }
                  if ((in_nodes[0]->read_output_value() == -9999) &&
                      (in_nodes[1]->read_output_value() != -9999) &&
                      (value != -9999))
                  {
                    float new_input = value - in_nodes[1]->read_output_value();
#ifdef DEBUG
                    cerr << "plus_constraint::propagate: node: "
                          << name << " setting input 0 to "
                          << new_input << "\n";
#endif
                    in_nodes[0]->set_output_value(new_input);
                  }
                  if ((in_nodes[1]->read_output_value() == -9999) &&
                      (in_nodes[0]->read_output_value() != -9999) &&
                      (value != -9999))
                  {
                    float new_input = value - in_nodes[0]->read_output_value();
#ifdef DEBUG
                    cerr << "plus_constraint::propagate: node: "
                          << name << " setting input 1 to "
                          << new_input << "\n";
#endif
                    in_nodes[1]->set_output_value(new_input);
                  }
                  return original_value - value;

            } else
                //
                // Here, we are in relaxation mode, so just calculate error.
                // The class constraint_collection member functions solve
                // and solve_by_relaxation use the error that is calculated
                // here to reduce the amount of error for all constraint
                // objects in the collection.
                //
                return (in_nodes[0]->read_output_value() +
                        in_nodes[1]->read_output_value())
                      - out_nodes[0]->read_original_value();
    }
```

The following listing of cnstrCol.cp shows the implementation of the class constraint_collection. This class did not exist in the first prototype implementation of the constraint library (as mentioned in Sec. 2.1, in the prototype implementation that is not shown here, I used static class variables in the base constraint class to keep track of and control all constraint objects). Using a separate container class with the constraint management behavior of the class constraint_collection allows you to use more than one independent constraint framework in your applications.

```
// File: cnstrCol.cp
//
// Description: The constraint_collection class acts as a normal
//              collection, and also provides the behavior of
//              constraint satisfaction networks.  An instance
//              of the constraint_collection class can solve
//              the constraint problem represented by the
//              contained constraint nodes by simple propagation
//              and by numerical relaxation.
//
//              constraint_collection is an abstract base class
//
//
// This software may be used without restriction in compiled form. This
// source code may not be redistributed without permission.
//
#include "cnstrCol.h"

//
//          Class constructor: constraint_collection
//

constraint_collection::constraint_collection()
{
  num_constraints = 0;
  random_sequence = new RandomSequence();
}


//
//          Class destructor: constraint_collection
//

constraint_collection::~constraint_collection()
{
  delete random_sequence;
}


//
//          Define operator[] for accessing constraint
//          collection elements
//

constraint & constraint_collection::operator[](int index)
{
  if (index < 0 || index >= num_constraints)
  {
    cerr << "constraint_collection::operator[]: illegal index: "
         << index << "\n";
    exit(1);
  }
   return *class_constraints[index];
}


//
//          Utility used in derived classes for
//          calculating the absolute value
//

float abs_value(float v)
{
  if (v >= 0.0)  return v;
  return -v;
}
```

The following listing of numCnCol.h shows the implementation of the num_con straint_collection class. This class was created when the behavior for solving numerical constraints was removed from the first prototype of the constraint_ collection_class.

```cpp
// File: numCnCol.h
//
// Description: The num_constraint_collection class acts as a normal
//              collection, and also provides the behavior of constraint
//              satisfaction networks for numerical (floating-point)
//              constraints.
//
//
// This software may be used without restriction in compiled form.
// This source code may not be redistributed without permission.
//
#include "numcncol.h"
//
//          Constant to set the maximum allowed number
//          of relaxation cycles:
//

const int MAX_DEPTH = 15;
//
//          Class constructor: num_constraint_collection
//

num_constraint_collection::num_constraint_collection()
            : constraint_collection()
{
#ifdef WINDOWS
  // If this is running as a Windows program, get heap memory:
  for (int i=0; i<MAX_NODES; i++)
  {
      r_handles[i] = GlobalAlloc(GMEM_FIXED, sizeof(double)*MAX_GRID);
      relaxation_values[i] = (float *)GlobalLock(r_handles[i]);
  }
#endif
}

//
//          Class destructor: num_constraint_collection
//

num_constraint_collection::~num_constraint_collection()
{
#ifdef WINDOWS
  // If this is running as a Windows program, release heap memory:
  for (int i=0; i<MAX_NODES; i++)
  {
      GlobalFree(r_handles[i]);
  }
#endif
}

//
//          Attempt to satisfy all constraints in the collection:
//

int num_constraint_collection::solve()
{
#ifdef DEBUG
  cerr << "Solve constraints for of all nodes "
```

```
                     << "derived from class 'constraint':\n\n";
#endif
  relaxation_mode_flag = 0;
  for (int i=0; i<num_constraints; i++)
  {
    class_constraints[i]->save_original_value();
  }

#ifdef DEBUG
  cerr << "...propagating constraints:\n";
#endif
  for (int relaxation_cycles=0; relaxation_cycles<3;
       relaxation_cycles++)
  {
    for (i=0; i<num_constraints; i++)
    {
      class_constraints[i]->propagate();
    }
  }

  // Test for cycles:
  num_relaxation_nodes = 0;
  for (i=0; i<num_constraints; i++)
  {
    if (class_constraints[i]->read_output_value() == -9999)
    {
#ifdef DEBUG
      cerr << "** node with a cycle: index: " << i
           << ", name: " << class_constraints[i]->>name << "\n";
#endif
      relaxation_node_indices[num_relaxation_nodes++] = i;
    }

  }
  if (num_relaxation_nodes > 0)
  {
#ifdef DEBUG
    cerr << "\nPerforming relaxation...\n\n";
#endif
    relaxation_mode_flag = 1;
    for (int depth=0; depth<MAX_DEPTH; depth++)
      solve_by_relaxation(depth);
  }
  return 0;
}

float abs_value(float v);

int num_constraint_collection::solve_by_relaxation(int depth)
{
    static float last_error = 999999999999999.99;
    int j;
#ifdef DEBUG
    cerr << "\nsolve_by_relaxation(" << depth << ")\n";
#endif
    int num_grid_points_per_var=MAX_GRID  /
        (num_relaxation_nodes*num_relaxation_nodes);

    int max_grid;
    if (num_relaxation_nodes == 1)
    {
      num_grid_points_per_var = 20;
    } else if (num_relaxation_nodes == 2)
    {
```

```
      num_grid_points_per_var = 16;
    } else if (num_relaxation_nodes == 3)
    {
    num_grid_points_per_var = 7;
    } else  if (num_relaxation_nodes == 4)
    {
    num_grid_points_per_var = 4;
    } else
    {
        cerr << "Illegal num_relaxation_nodes= "
            << num_relaxation_nodes << "\n";
        exit(0);
    }
    max_grid = 1;
  for (int nr=0; nr<num_relaxation_nodes; nr++)
    max_grid *= num_grid_points_per_var;
      if (max_grid > MAX_GRID)
  {
    cerr << "Illegal: num_constraint_collection::"
        << "solve_by_relaxation: max_grid= " << max_grid << "\n";
    exit(1);
  }

#ifdef DEBUG
  cerr << "num_relaxation_nodes= " << num_relaxation_nodes
      << ", num_grid_points_per_var= " << num_grid_points_per_var
      << ", max_grid= " << max_grid << "\n";
#endif
        float spacing = 1.0 / ((float)(num_grid_points_per_var-1));

    if (depth == 0)
    {
      for (int k=0; k<MAX_NODES; k++)
      {
        v_min[k] = -600.0;
        v_max[k] =  1000.0;
      }
    }

#ifdef DEBUG
    for (j=0; j<num_relaxation_nodes; j++)
    {
      cerr << " v_min[" << j << "] = " << v_min[j] << "\n";
      cerr << " v_max[" << j << "] = " << v_max[j] << "\n\n";
    }
#endif

    float v_delta[MAX_NODES];

    for (int i=0; i<num_relaxation_nodes; i++)
    {
        v_delta[i] = abs_value(v_max[i] - v_min[i]) * spacing;
    }

    for (j=0; j<max_grid; j++)
    {

        for (int m=0; m<num_relaxation_nodes; m++)
        {
            relaxation_values[m][j] =
                random_sequence->rndFP(v_min[m], v_max[m]);
        }
    }
```

```
      // loop over each grid combination:
   for (int grid_index=0; grid_index<max_grid; grid_index++)
   {
     relaxation_error[grid_index] = 0.0;
     for (int mm=0; mm<num_constraints; mm++)
     {
       class_constraints[mm]->reset_to_original_value();
     }

     for (int relax_index=0; relax_index<num_relaxation_nodes; relax_index++)
     {              int index = relaxation_node_indices[relax_index];
                    class_constraints[index]->

     set_output_value(relaxation_values[relax_index][grid_index]);
     }
            // propagate values, and calculate error on 'constant' terms:
     float error = 0.0;
     for (int relaxation_cycles=0; relaxation_cycles<1; relaxation_cycles++)
     {
       for (int ii=0; ii<num_constraints; ii++)
       {
         error += abs_value(class_constraints[ii]->propagate());
       }
     }
     relaxation_error[grid_index] += error;
   }

   // find the best guess:
   int best_index = 0;
   float best_error = relaxation_error[0];
   for (grid_index=1; grid_index<max_grid; grid_index++)
   {
     if (relaxation_error[grid_index] < best_error)
     {
       best_error = relaxation_error[grid_index];
       best_index = grid_index;
     }
   }

#ifdef DEBUG
   cerr << " * *  best_index= " << best_index
        << ", best_error= " << best_error <<" * *\n";
   for (int kk=0; kk<num_relaxation_nodes; kk++)
   {
     cerr << "best val[" << kk << "]= "
          << relaxation_values[kk][best_index] << " ";
   }
   cerr << "\n";
#endif

   // Recalculate the v_min[] and v_max[] arrays, each "band" being centered
   // on the best value so far for its corresponding relaxation variable:
   // Note: we are using a greedy algorithm, which will sometimes reduce the
   //       search range for a given relaxation variable past an optimal
   //       value.  A simple heuristic is to occasionally increase the
   //       search interval:
     static float save_best_values[MAX_NODES];
     // don't change search widths if error does not improve:
   if (best_error < 0.5 * last_error && depth > 3)
   {
     cerr << "!! narrowing search width...\n";
     float sqrt_error = sqrt(best_error);
     cerr << "sqrt of best error = " << sqrt_error << "\n";
```

```
            last_error = best_error;
            for (int ll=0; ll<num_relaxation_nodes; ll++)
            {
                save_best_values[ll] = relaxation_values[ll][best_index];
                float width;
                        width = 3.5*sqrt_error;
                if (width < 3.0)  width *= 1.5;
                v_min[ll] = relaxation_values[ll][best_index] - width/2.0;
                v_max[ll] = v_min[ll] + width;
            }
            last_error = best_error;
        }  else
        {
            // in case we get a very low error early on which locks us out:
            last_error *= 1.2;
            if (best_error < 0.7 * last_error)
            {
              cerr << "normal width reduction, last_error = " << last_error
                    << ", current best_error = " << best_error << "\n";
              last_error = best_error;
              for (int ll=0; ll<num_relaxation_nodes; ll++)
              {
                float width =3.5 * abs_value(v_delta[ll])
                            * (float)num_relaxation_nodes;
                v_min[ll] = relaxation_values[ll][best_index] - width/2.0;
                v_max[ll] = v_min[ll] + width;
              }
            }
        }

    // print out relaxation data for debugging:
#ifdef DEBUG
        cerr << "\n------- Relaxation data:\n\n";
        for (int relax_index=0; relax_index<num_relaxation_nodes; relax_index++)
        {
          int index = relaxation_node_indices[relax_index];
          cerr << "Node: " << class_constraints[index]->name << "\n";
          for (int grid_index=0; grid_index<max_grid; grid_index++)
          {
            cerr << " relaxation_values[" << relax_index
                << "][" << grid_index << "] = "
                << relaxation_values[relax_index][grid_index] << ",
                error = " << relaxation_error[grid_index] << "\n";
          }
        }
#endif
        if (depth > (MAX_DEPTH - 10))
        {
          for (int ri=0; ri<num_relaxation_nodes; ri++)
          {
            int index = relaxation_node_indices[ri];
            class_constraints[index]->set_output_value(save_best_values[ri]);
          }
        }
    }

    return 0;
}
```

In Sec. 3.4, I give the implementation of classes `geometric_constraint` and `geometric_constraint_collection`, which demonstrate how we easily implement constraint satisfaction using constraint objects with more complex data structures.

3

Application Example: Placing Furniture in a Room Subject to Specified Constraints

Now let's write an application that solves an interesting class of problems: placing geometric objects in a space subject to stated constraints. We'll use the physical metaphor of placing pieces of furniture in a room. You will see how to extend the C++ constraint library by subclassing to solve other similar types of layout problems. This furniture placement problem can be solved easily by defining the new C++ classes `geometric_constraint` and `geometric_constraint_collection`. This new subclass will be further subclassed to solve different varieties of placement problems.

The `geometric_constraint_collection` class contains `geometric_constraint` objects. The `geometric_constraint_collection` class re-arranges the locations of the `geometric_constraint` objects that it contains to meet two constraints:

1. `geometric_constraint` objects do not overlap
2. all `geometric_constraint` objects are located inside a bounding rectangle

3.1 The Geometric Constraint Class

I want to design the `geometric_constraint` class so that it has data defining a two-dimensional rectangular "enclosure" area, and behavior such that no two `geometric_constraint` objects are allowed to "overlap" if they belong to the same `geometric_constraint_collection`. This is certainly the kind of behavior I would want for furniture objects!

You will probably want to extend the `constraint` class library for solving other types of applications. We will subclass the `variable_constraint` and `constant_constraint` classes in Chapter 4 for use in an investment planning system.

3.2 Class Structure for Geometric Constraint Classes

The `constraint` collection class was subclassed in Chapter 2 to provide constraint services for numerical data items. In this chapter, we subclass the `constraint` collection to provide constraint services for geometric objects that are bounded by a rectangle.

3.3 Geometric Constraint Class Interfaces

In Secs. 2.3 and 2.4 I derived the `constraint` collection class `num_constraint_collection` from `constraint_collection`, adding behavior for solving numerical constraint problems. Now I derive geometric constraint classes to add behavior for solving geometric constraint problems.

The following listing shows the class interface for a geometric constraint object.

```
// File: geom.h
//
// Description: This file contains the C++ interface for the class
//              geometric_constraint, and is derived from class constraint.
//              This class constrains the position of the constraint object
//              not to overlap other constraint objects in the
//              constraint collection that contains it.
//
//
// This software may be used without restriction in compiled form.
// This source code may not be redistributed without permission.
//
#ifndef __geometric
#define __geometric
#include "constrn.h"

#include <iostream.h>

#include <math.h>

const int GEOM_TYPE = 3124;

const int GEOM_MAX_GRID = 256;

class constraint_collection;

class geometric_constraint : public constraint {
 public:
  geometric_constraint(const char *my_name = "no_name");
  float propagate();
  virtual int my_type() { return GEOM_TYPE; }
  void set_bounding_box(float new_x_min, float new_x_max,
                        float new_y_min, float new_y_max);
  void get_bounding_box(float &new_x_min, float &new_x_max,
                        float &new_y_min, float &new_y_max);
  void set_new_origin(float new_x, float new_y);
  void rotate_90_degrees();  // about the origin
```

```
float get_x_min() { return x_min; }
float get_x_max() { return x_max; }
float get_y_min() { return y_min; }
float get_y_max() { return y_max; }

protected:
  // coordinates for bounding box assumed to be aligned with
  // Cartesian coordinate system:
  float x_min;
  float x_max;
  float y_min;
  float y_max;

  float overlap(geometric_constraint &gc);

};

#endif
```

The class `geometric_constraint` adds member data for defining the bounding rectangle of a geometric object. The bounding box is represented by minimum and maximum x-y coordinates. When an instance of the `geometric_constraint` class is placed in a `geometric_constraint_collection` (in Figure 3.1, a `geometric_`

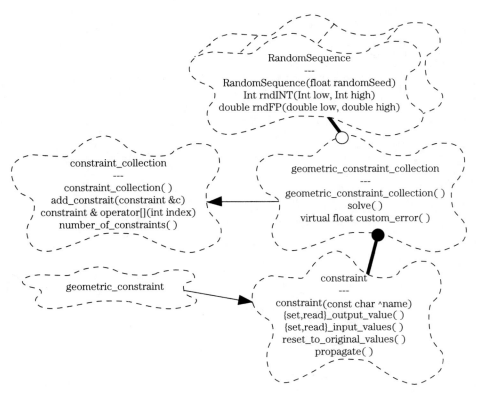

Figure 3.1 Constraint classes for geometric shapes.

constraint_collection contains zero or more constraint objects), its bounding box will stay the same size, but can be moved when the geometric_constraint_collection rearranges geometric objects to solve geometric constraint problems.

The virtual member function my_type returns an integer object type that is used by a geometric constraint collection to determine which constraint objects that it contains are geometric constraint objects; nongeometric constraint objects are ignored by the collection.

The following listing shows the interface for the geometric constraint collection class.

```
// File: geomCol.h
//
// Description: The constraint_collection class acts as a normal collection,
//              and also provides the behavior of constraint satisfaction
//              networks.  An instance of the constraint_collection class can
//              solve the constraint problem represented by the contained
//              constraint nodes by simple propagation, graph rewriting to
//              eliminate cycles, and numerical relaxation.
//
//
// This software may be used without restriction in compiled form.
// This source code may not be redistributed without permission.
//
#ifndef geomCol_h
#define geomCol_h

#include "cnstrcol.h"
#include "geom.h"

class geometric_constraint_collection : public constraint_collection
 {
 public:
    geometric_constraint_collection();
    ~geometric_constraint_collection();
    void set_bounding_area(float new_x_min, float new_x_max,
                           float new_y_min, float new_y_max);
    void get_bounding_area(float &ret_x_min, float &ret_x_max,
                           float &ret_y_min, float &ret_y_max);

    float get_x_min() { return x_min; }
    float get_x_max() { return x_max; }
    float get_y_min() { return y_min; }
    float get_y_max() { return y_max; }

    int solve();

    int print_solution();

 protected:

    // to customize ranking in sub-classes:
    virtual float custom_error();

    float x_min;
    float x_max;
    float y_min;
    float y_max;

#ifndef WINDOWS
    float relaxation_values_x[MAX_NODES][GEOM_MAX_GRID];
```

```
        float relaxation_values_y[MAX_NODES][GEOM_MAX_GRID];
        unsigned char rotation_flags[MAX_NODES][GEOM_MAX_GRID];
#else
        float FAR * relaxation_values_x[MAX_NODES];
        HANDLE r_handles_x[MAX_NODES];
        float FAR * relaxation_values_y[MAX_NODES];
        HANDLE r_handles_y[MAX_NODES];
        unsigned char FAR * rotation_flags[MAX_NODES];
        HANDLE r_handles_rotation_flags[MAX_NODES];
#endif

 private:
        int solve_by_relaxation(int depth);
        int best_index;
        float best_error;

};

#endif
```

The `geometric_constraint_collection` is derived from class `constraint_ collection` and adds behavior for solving geometric constraint problems. Like `geometric_constraint` objects, instances of the class `geometric_constraint_ collection` have member data that defines a bounding box; that box is used to define the area in which contained `geometric_constraint` objects are placed when the member function `solve` is executed. The member function `print_solution` is a utility to print out the names and locations of all `geometric_constraint` objects contained in the collection.

3.4 Implementation of the Geometric Constraint Classes

The following listing shows the implementation of the `geometric_constraint` class.

```
// File: geom.cp
//
// Description: This file contains the C++ implementation for
//              class geometric_constraint.
//
//
// This software may be used without restriction in compiled form.
// This source code can not be redistributed without permission.
//
#include "geom.h"
#include "cnstrCol.h"

//
//          Class constructor: geometric_constraint
//

geometric_constraint::geometric_constraint(const char *my_name)
        : constraint(my_name)
{
#ifdef DEBUG
  cerr << "entering derived class 'geometric_constraint' constructor: "
       << my_name << "\n";
#endif
```

```
}

//
//          Utilities for setting and getting the
//          bounding box for a geometric_constraint
//          object:

void geometric_constraint::set_bounding_box(float new_x_min,
                                            float new_x_max,
                                            float new_y_min,
                                            float new_y_max)
{
    x_min = new_x_min;   x_max = new_x_max;
    y_min = new_y_min;   y_max = new_y_max;
}

void geometric_constraint::get_bounding_box(float &return_x_min,
                                            float &return_x_max,
                                            float &return_y_min,
                                            float &return_y_max)
{
    return_x_min = x_min;   return_x_max = x_max;
    return_y_min = y_min;   return_y_max = y_max;
}

//
//          Private member function to calculate overlap
//          with another geometric_constraint object:
//

float geometric_constraint::overlap(geometric_constraint &gc)
{
    float ret_val;
    float x_overlap = 0;
    // "this" object to the left of "gc":
    if (get_x_min() < gc.get_x_min())
    {          x_overlap = get_x_max() - gc.get_x_min();
    } else
    {  // "this" object to the right of "gc":
        x_overlap = gc.get_x_max() - get_x_min();
    }
    if (x_overlap < 0.0)   x_overlap = 0.0;

    float y_overlap = 0;
    // "this" object is below "gc":
    if (get_y_min() < gc.get_y_min())
    {          y_overlap = get_y_max() - gc.get_y_min();
    } else
    {  // "this" object is above "gc":
        y_overlap = gc.get_y_max() - get_y_min();
    }
    if (y_overlap < 0.0)   y_overlap = 0.0;

    ret_val = x_overlap * y_overlap;

    return ret_val;
}

//
//          Member function propagate calculates the error
//          associated with this object overlapping with
//          any other geometric_constraint object contained
//          in the same container:
//
```

```
float geometric_constraint::propagate()
{
  if (my_container == NULL) {
      cerr << "NULL my_container pointer in "
           << "geometric_constraint::propagate\n";
      exit(1);
  }

  // we are in relaxation mode, so just calculate error due to
  // overlap of other geometric_constraint objects in the
  // collection which contains this object:

  float ret_val = 0.0;

  for (int i=0; i<container()->get_num_constraints(); i++)
  {
      if ((*(container()))[i].my_type() == GEOM_TYPE &&
          &((*(container()))[i]) != this)
      {
            constraint_collection *c = container();
            geometric_constraint *gc =
                (geometric_constraint *)&((*c)[i]);
            ret_val += 1000.0 * overlap(*gc);
      }
  }
  return ret_val;
}

//
//          Member function: set_new_origin
//

void geometric_constraint::set_new_origin(float new_x, float new_y)
{
    float x_delta = x_min - new_x;
    float y_delta = y_min - new_y;
    x_min -= x_delta;
    x_max -= x_delta;
    y_min -= y_delta;
    y_max -= y_delta;
}

//
//          Member function rotate_90_degrees rotates
//          a geometric constraint object about the
//          point (x_min, y_min):
//

void geometric_constraint::rotate_90_degrees()
{
    float x_max_save = x_max;
    x_max = y_max;
    y_max = x_max_save;
}
```

The geometric_constraint member function overlap is a utility function that calculates the amount of overlap between two geometric_constraint objects. The member function propagate sums the total error of the overlap between a geometric_constraint object and all other geometric_constraint objects contained in the same geometric_constraint_collection object.

The following listing shows the implementation of the geometric constraint collection class.

```
// File: geomCol.cp
//
// Description: This file contains the C++ implementation of the
//              class geometric_constraint_collection.
//
//
// This software may be used without restriction in compiled form.
// This source code may not be redistributed without permission.
//
#include "geomCol.h"

//
//          Set the maximum number of relaxation cycles
//          used in member function solve.  This value
//          controls how well geometric constraint objects
//          are arranged.
//

const int MAX_DEPTH = 30;

float abs_value(float v);

//
//          Class constructor: geometric_constraint_collection
//

geometric_constraint_collection::geometric_constraint_collection()
            : constraint_collection()
{
#ifdef WINDOWS
  // For Windows only: allocate large data structures on
  // the Windows heap:
  for (int i=0; i<MAX_NODES; i++)
  {
    r_handles_x[i] =
          GlobalAlloc(GMEM_FIXED, sizeof(float)*GEOM_MAX_GRID);
    r_handles_y[i] =
          GlobalAlloc(GMEM_FIXED, sizeof(float)*GEOM_MAX_GRID);
    r_handles_rotation_flags[i] =
          GlobalAlloc(GMEM_FIXED, sizeof(unsigned char)*GEOM_MAX_GRID);

    relaxation_values_x[i] = (float FAR *)GlobalLock(r_handles_x[i]);
    relaxation_values_y[i] = (float FAR *)GlobalLock(r_handles_y[i]);
    rotation_flags[i] =
          (unsigned char FAR *)GlobalLock(r_handles_rotation_flags[i]);
  }
#endif
}

//
//          Class constructor: geometric_constraint_collection
//

geometric_constraint_collection::~geometric_constraint_collection()
{
#ifdef WINDOWS
    // For Windows only: deallocate large data structures from
    // the Windows heap:
    for (int i=0; i<MAX_NODES; i++)
    {
```

```
        GlobalFree(r_handles_x[i]);
        GlobalFree(r_handles_y[i]);
        GlobalFree(r_handles_rotation_flags[i]);
    }
#endif
}

//
//          Member function to set the bounding area
//          inside which all contained geometric_constraint
//          objects will be arranged (if possible) when
//          member function solve is called.
//

void geometric_constraint_collection::set_bounding_area
            (float new_x_min, float new_x_max,
             float new_y_min, float new_y_max)
{
    x_min = new_x_min;    x_max = new_x_max;
    y_min = new_y_min;    y_max = new_y_max;
}

//
//          Get the current bounding area box:
//

void geometric_constraint_collection::get_bounding_area
            (float &ret_x_min, float &ret_x_max,
             float &ret_y_min, float &ret_y_max)
{
    ret_x_min = x_min;    ret_x_max = x_max;
    ret_y_min = y_min;    ret_y_max = y_max;
}

//
//          Attempt to arrange all of the geometric_constraint
//          objects contained in this collection inside the
//          bounding area set for this collection.
//

int geometric_constraint_collection::solve()
{
    relaxation_mode_flag = 1;
    // All geometric constraints are relaxation constraints:
    num_relaxation_nodes = get_num_constraints();
    best_index = -1;
    for (int depth=0; depth<MAX_DEPTH; depth++)  {
        if (solve_by_relaxation(depth) == 0) break;
    }

    for (int mm=0; mm<num_relaxation_nodes; mm++)
    {
        if (class_constraints[mm]->my_type() == GEOM_TYPE)
        {
            geometric_constraint *gc =
                (geometric_constraint *)class_constraints[mm];
            gc->set_new_origin(relaxation_values_x[mm][best_index],
                               relaxation_values_y[mm][best_index]);

        }
    }
    if (best_error < 0.01)
        return TRUE;  // solved
    else
```

```
                return FALSE;
}

int geometric_constraint_collection::solve_by_relaxation(int depth)
{

#ifdef DEBUG
    cerr << "\nsolve_by_relaxation(" << depth << ")\n";
#endif

    int num_grid_points_per_var =
        GEOM_MAX_GRID/(num_relaxation_nodes*num_relaxation_nodes);

    int max_grid;

    switch (num_relaxation_nodes)
    {
      case 1:
            num_grid_points_per_var = 128;
            break;

      case 2:
            num_grid_points_per_var =7;
            break;

      case 3:
            num_grid_points_per_var = 5;
            break;

      case 4:
            num_grid_points_per_var = 3;
            break;

      default:
            cerr << "Illegal num_relaxation_nodes= "
                << num_relaxation_nodes << "\n";
            exit(0);
    }

    max_grid = 1;
    for (int nr=0; nr<num_relaxation_nodes; nr++)
        max_grid *= num_grid_points_per_var;
        if (max_grid > GEOM_MAX_GRID) {
        cerr << "Illegal: constraint_collection::solve_by_relaxation"
            << ": max_grid= " << max_grid << "\n";
        exit(1);
    }

#ifdef DEBUG
    cerr << "num_relaxation_nodes= " << num_relaxation_nodes
        << ", num_grid_points_per_var= " << num_grid_points_per_var
        << ", max_grid= " << max_grid << ", best_index="
        << best_index << "\n";
#endif

    for (int j=0; j<max_grid; j++)
    {
        for (int m=0; m<num_relaxation_nodes; m++)
        {
            // Do not overwrite the best trial from the
            // last iteration:
            if (j != best_index)
            {
                geometric_constraint * gc =
```

```
                               (geometric_constraint *)class_constraints[m];
                   float x_width = gc->get_x_max() - gc->get_x_min();
                   float y_width = gc->get_y_max() - gc->get_y_min();
                   relaxation_values_x[m][j] =
                           random_sequence->rndFP(x_min, x_max - x_width);
                   relaxation_values_y[m][j] =
                           random_sequence->rndFP(y_min, y_max - y_width);
                   rotation_flags[m][j] = 0;   // NO ROTATION (Yet!!)
               }
           }
       }

        // loop over each grid combination:
       for (int grid_index=0; grid_index<max_grid; grid_index++)
       {
         relaxation_error[grid_index] = 0.0;
         for (int mm=0; mm<num_relaxation_nodes; mm++)
         {
           if (class_constraints[mm]->my_type() == GEOM_TYPE)
           {
               geometric_constraint *gc =
                       (geometric_constraint *)class_constraints[mm];
               gc->set_new_origin(relaxation_values_x[mm][grid_index],
                               relaxation_values_y[mm][grid_index]);
           }
         }

         // propagate values, and calculate error on 'constant' terms:
         float error = 0.0;
         for (int ii=0; ii<num_constraints; ii++)
             error += abs_value(class_constraints[ii]->propagate());

         // The member function custom_error returns 0.0 for this class,
         // but is virtual and can be defined in subclasses to change
         // the ranking order of relaxation samples:

         relaxation_error[grid_index] += error + custom_error();
       }

       // find the best guess:
       best_error = relaxation_error[0];
       for (grid_index=1; grid_index<max_grid; grid_index++)
       {
         if (relaxation_error[grid_index] < best_error)
         {
           best_error = relaxation_error[grid_index];
           best_index = grid_index;
         }
       }

#ifdef DEBUG
    print_solution();
#endif

    int ret_val = 0;
    // not done with search:
    if (abs_value(best_error) > 0.00001)  ret_val = 1;
return ret_val;
}


//
//          Class utility function to print out parameters
//          for this class and all contained constraint
//          objects.
```

```
//
int geometric_constraint_collection::print_solution()
{
    if (best_index == -1)  return FALSE;
    cerr << "\nRoom width: " << (get_x_max() - get_x_min())
        << ", room height: " << (get_y_max() - get_y_min());

    cerr << "\n\nBest solution found:\n\n";

    cerr <<"Parameters:  best_index= " << best_index
        << ", best_error= " < best_error <<"\n";

    for (int mm=0; mm<num_relaxation_nodes; mm++)
    {
        if (class_constraints[mm]->my_type() == GEOM_TYPE)
        {
            geometric_constraint *gc =
                    (geometric_constraint *)class_constraints[mm];
            cerr << "\n    Name: " << gc->name << "\n\n";
            cerr << "      x_min, x_max: " << gc->get_x_min()
                << ", " << gc->get_x_max() << "\n";
            cerr << "      y_min, y_max: " << gc->get_y_min()
                << ", " << gc->get_y_max() << "\n";
        }
    }

    return TRUE;
}

//
//          Virtual member function: custom_error
//
//          NOTE: redefine this function in derived
//                classes to change the packing
//                behavior in member function solve.
//

float geometric_constraint_collection::custom_error()
{
    return 0.0;
}
```

The geometric_constraint_collection member function solve rearranges the geometric_constraint objects contained in the collection so that all of the objects fit within the bounding box set for the collection. The member function print_solution is a utility for printing the names and locations of all geometric constraint objects in the collection.

The virtual member function custom_error simply returns a value of zero for class geometric_constraint_collection. When new classes are derived, this member function is a convenient way to override or augment the behavior for arranging geometric constraint objects.

3.5 Example Using the Geometric Constraint Classes

Geometric constraint collection objects have instance variables that specify a bounding box region that contains all contained geometric constraint objects. For this example, I create one geometric constraint collection object and set this bounding region to the size of a room. I then create several geometric constraint objects representing pieces of furniture, and ask the geometric constraint collection to move the furniture objects until they do not overlap.

The following listing shows how to set up and solve this simple problem.

```
// File: test.cp
//
// Description: This file contains a simple test program for the
//              geometric constraint classes.
//

#include "constrn.h"
#include "plus.h"
#include "multiply.h"
#include "constant.h"
#include "variable.h"
#include "geomCol.h"

const float room_width = 12.0;
const float room_length= 20.0;

const float couch_width = 3.5;
const float couch_length= 9.8;

const float coffee_table_width = 2.2;
const float coffee_table_length=6.0;

const float table_width = 5.0;
const float table_length= 7.0;

void main()
{
  cerr << "Use geometric constraint class to place furniture\n";

  geometric_constraint_collection cc;

  geometric_constraint couch("couch");
  couch.set_bounding_box(0.0, couch_width, 0.0, couch_length);

  geometric_constraint coffee_table("coffee_table");
  coffee_table.set_bounding_box(0.0, coffee_table_width,
                                0.0, coffee_table_length);
  geometric_constraint table("table");
  table.set_bounding_box(0.0, table_width, 0.0, table_length);

  cc.add_constraint(couch);
  cc.add_constraint(coffee_table);
  cc.add_constraint(table);

  cc.set_bounding_area(0.0, room_width, 0.0, room_length);

  cc.solve();

  cc.print_solution();

}
```

In this example program, I define the room dimensions and the sizes of three pieces of furniture. I create a new geometric_constraint_collection object cc and add the three furniture objects to it. The geometric_constraint_collection class member functions `solve` and `print_solution` are called to find and print a solution, as seen in the following listing.

```
Use geometric constraint class to place furniture
Room width: 12, room height: 20

Best solution found:

Parameters:  best_index= 37, best_error= 0

For couch:
best val X[0]= 6.0706
best val Y[0]= 0.207549

For coffee_table:
best val X[1]= 1.307709
best val Y[1]= 3.254496

For table:
best val X[2]= 3.454787
best val Y[2]= 12.873671
```

Notice that the value for best error is zero. The class `geometric_constraint_collection` class member function `solve` calculated a zero error for this layout of the `geometric_constraint` objects couch, coffee_table, and table because all of the constraints were met exactly. In Sec. 3.6, I override member function `custom_error` to introduce small errors, which will bias the placement of contained `geometric_constraint` objects. The error introduced by function `custom_error` will always be small, so that the higher priority constraints of nonoverlapping objects and placement within the constraint collection's bounding area are always satisfied before the finer-grained constraints introduced in collection class member function `custom_error`.

Figure 3.2 shows a typical arrangement of constraint objects produced by this test program.

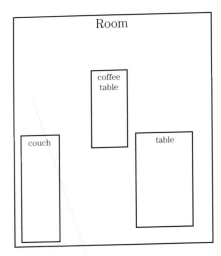

Figure 3.2 The `geometric_constraint_collection` class arranges contained objects so that they do not overlap.

3.6 Adding Dense and Loose Packing Behavior

The example in Sec. 3.5 was not too interesting because it simply fits all geometric constraint objects into a bounded area. In this section, I add three new subclasses to `geometric_constraint_collection` to add behavior for calculating how tightly objects are packed together, and for setting a preference for loose packing and tight packing of geometric objects within a bounded region. Figure 3.3 shows the classes from Figure 3.1 and the three new classes.

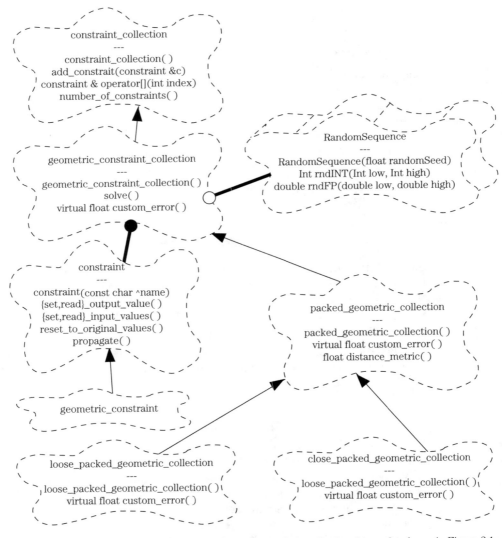

Figure 3-3 Three additional geometric constraint classes added to the class hierarchy shown in Figure 3.1: `packed_geometric_collection`,   `loose_packed_geom_collection`,   `close_packed_geom_collection`.

The following listing shows the interface for the `packed_geometric_collec`
`tion` class.

```
// File: pkgeocol.h
//
// Description: The packed_geometric_collection is derived from
//              class geometric_constraint_collection and adds the
//              ability to calculate how closely packed contained
//              geometric constraint objects are.
//
//
// This software may be used without restriction in compiled form.
// This source code can not be redistributed without permission.
//
#ifndef PkGeoCol_h
#define PkGeoCol_h

#include "geomCol.h"
#include "geom.h"

class packed_geometric_collection : public geometric_constraint_collection {
  public:
      packed_geometric_collection();
     ~packed_geometric_collection();
      virtual float custom_error() = 0;  // Abstract base class
      float distance_metric();
};

#endif
```

The class `packed_geometric_collection` adds two interesting new behaviors
to its base class `geometric_collection`:

- member function `custom_error` can perform any desired calculation based on
  the current state of the `geometric_constraint` objects contained in the collection that can affect the ranking of solutions satisfying the higher-priority constraints of nonoverlapping objects and all objects being contained inside the
  constraint collection's bounding area

- member function `distance_metric` calculates a numerical value characterizing
  how close objects in the collection are to each other

Also note that this is an abstract base class.

Abstract base classes in C++

In C++, a base class is used to provide default behavior and data structures
that can be inherited by derived classes. When you design a new C++ class that
is very abstract, you might want to force programmers who are using your C++
class to derive a new class. In other words, you might want to make it illegal to
create instances of a class; the compiler will report a fatal compilation error if
you then try to create instances of an abstract base class.

I create an abstract base class by defining a virtual function and setting it to
zero in the class definition. The following is illegal:

```
class packed_geometric_collection : public
geometric_constraint_collection {
 public:
     packed_geometric_collection();
    ~packed_geometric_collection();
     virtual float custom_error() = 0;  // Abstract base class
     float distance_metric();
};

packed_geometric_collection pgc;  // illegal!
```

Declaring abstract classes as abstract base classes reminds users of your class that you intend it to be subclassed with supplemental data and behavior added.

The following listing shows the C++ interface for the `loose_packed_geom_collection` class:

```
// File: loosePk.h
//
// Description: The packed_geometric_collection is derived from
//              class geometric_constraint_collection and adds the
//              ability to calculate how closely packed contained
//              geometric constraint objects are.
//
//              The loose_packed_geom_collection class is derived
//              from the packed_geometric_collection and adds the
//              behavior of organizing contained geometric constraint
//              objects so that they are as far apart as possible,
//              while still meeting the constraint of being contained
//              within a bounding rectangle and not overlapping.
//
//
// This software may be used without restriction in compiled form.
// This source code may not be redistributed without permission.
//
#ifndef loosePk_h
#define loosePk_h

#include "PkGeoCol.h"
#include "geom.h"

class loose_packed_geom_collection :
 public packed_geometric_collection {
 public:
     loose_packed_geom_collection();
    ~loose_packed_geom_collection();
     virtual float custom_error();
};

#endif
```

In class `loose_packed_collection`, I derive a new class from the abstract base class `packed_geom_collection` that defines the virtual member function `custom_error` so that it returns a smaller error if the constraint objects in the `loose_packed_geom_collection` are far apart. In calculating this error value, member function `custom_error` uses the member function `distance_metric` inherited from its base class `packed_geom_collection`.

The following listing shows the C++ interface for the `tight_packed_geom_collection` class.

```
// File: tightPk.h
//
// Description: The packed_geometric_collection is derived from
//              class geometric_constraint_collection and adds the
//              ability to calculate how closely packed contained
//              geometric constraint objects are.
//
//              The tight_packed_geom_collection class is derived
//              from the packed_geometric_collection and adds the
//              behavior of organizing contained geometric constraint
//              objects so that they are as close together as possible,
//              while still meeting the constraint of being contained
//              within a bounding rectangle and not overlapping.
//
//
// This software may be used without restriction in compiled form.
// This source code can not be redistributed without permission.
//
#ifndef tightPk_h
#define tightPk_h

#include "PkGeoCol.h"
#include "geom.h"

class tight_packed_geom_collection :
 public packed_geometric_collection {
 public:
     tight_packed_geom_collection();
    ~tight_packed_geom_collection();
     virtual float custom_error();
};

#endif
```

In class `tight_packed_collection`, I derive a new class from the abstract base class `packed_geom_collection` that defines the virtual member function `cus tom_error` so that it returns a smaller error if the constraint objects in the `tight_packed_geom_collection` are close to each other. In calculating this error value, member function `custom_error` uses the member function `distance_metric` inherited from its base class `packed_geom_collection`.

The following listing shows the implementation for the packed_geometric_collection class.

```
// File: pkgeocol.cp
//
// Description: This file contains the C++ implementation of the
//              class packed_geometric_collection.
//
//
// This software may be used without restriction in compiled form.
// This source code may not be redistributed without permission.
//
#include "PkGeoCol.h"

//
//         Class constructor: packed_geometric_collection
```

```
//

packed_geometric_collection::packed_geometric_collection()
          : geometric_constraint_collection()
{
}


//
//          Class destructor: packed_geometric_collection
//

packed_geometric_collection::~packed_geometric_collection()
{
}


//
//          Member function: distance_metric
//
//          This function returns
//
//             sqrt(sum of squares of distances from centers)
//
//          This is of how close the objects in the collection
//          are to each other (i.e., a small value means that
//          the objects are close together)
//

float packed_geometric_collection::distance_metric()
{

    float ret_val = 0.0;
    for (int m=0; m<(num_relaxation_nodes - 1); m++)
    {
        if (class_constraints[m]->my_type() == GEOM_TYPE)
        {
            geometric_constraint *gc_1 =
                (geometric_constraint *)class_constraints[m];
            float x_center_1 =
                (gc_1->get_x_min() + gc_1->get_x_max())
                            / 2.0;
            float y_center_1 =
                (gc_1->get_y_min() + gc_1->get_y_max())
                            / 2.0;
            for (int i=m+1; i<num_relaxation_nodes; i++)
            {
                if (class_constraints[i]->my_type() == GEOM_TYPE)
                {
                    geometric_constraint *gc_2 =
                        (geometric_constraint *)class_constraints[i];
                    float x_center_2 =
                        (gc_2->get_x_min() + gc_2->get_x_max()) / 2.0;
                    float y_center_2 =
                        (gc_2->get_y_min() + gc_2->get_y_max()) / 2.0;
                    float del_x = (x_center_1 - x_center_2);
                    float del_y = (y_center_1 - y_center_2);
                    ret_val += del_x*del_x + del_y*del_y;
                }
            }
        }
    }

    return sqrt(ret_val);
}
```

The following listing shows the C++ implementation for the `loose_packed_geom_collection` class.

```
// File: loosePk.cp
//
// Description: This file contains the C++ implementation of the
//              class loose_packed_geom_collection.
//
//

#include "loosePk.h"

void pause();
float abs_value(float v);
extern "C" { void exit(int); };

loose_packed_geom_collection::loose_packed_geom_collection()
          : packed_geometric_collection()
{
}

loose_packed_geom_collection::~loose_packed_geom_collection()
{
}

// sqrt(sum of squares of distances from centers):
float loose_packed_geom_collection::custom_error()
{
    float ret_val = distance_metric() * 0.000001;
    ret_val = 0.025 - ret_val;
    if (ret_val < 0.0)  ret_val = 0.0;
    return ret_val;
}
```

The following listing shows the C++ implementation for the `tight_packed_geom_collection` class.

```
// File: tightPk.cp
//
// Description: This file contains the C++ implementation of the
//              class tight_packed_geom_collection.
//
//

#include "tightPk.h"

void pause();
float abs_value(float v);

extern "C" { void exit(int); };

tight_packed_geom_collection::tight_packed_geom_collection()
          : packed_geometric_collection()
{
}

tight_packed_geom_collection::~tight_packed_geom_collection()
{
}
```

```
// sqrt(sum of squares of distances from centers):
float tight_packed_geom_collection::custom_error()
{
    float ret_val = distance_metric() * 0.00001;
    return ret_val;
}
```

3.7 Testing Dense and Loose Packing Behavior

I use two short sample programs that were derived from the file test.cp listed in Sec. 3.5. The first listing in this section substitutes a `loose_packed_geom_collec tion` object for a `geometric_constraint_collection`. Using the same test data as the test program in Sec. 3.5, the following listing (file testa.cp in the ch3 directory on the software disk) places constraint objects as far apart as possible.

```
// File: testA.cp
//
// Description: Test the loose packing geometric
//              constraint collection class

#include "loosePk.h"

const float room_width = 12.0;
const float room_length= 20.0;

const float couch_width = 3.5;
const float couch_length= 9.8;

const float coffee_table_width = 2.2;
const float coffee_table_length=6.0;

const float table_width = 5.0;
const float table_length= 7.0;

void main()
{
  cerr << "Use loose packed geometric constraint class"
       << " to place furniture\n";

  loose_packed_geom_collection cc;

  geometric_constraint couch("couch");
  couch.set_bounding_box(0.0, couch_width, 0.0, couch_length);

  geometric_constraint coffee_table("coffee_table");
  coffee_table.set_bounding_box(0.0, coffee_table_width,
                                0.0, coffee_table_length);
  geometric_constraint table("table");
  table.set_bounding_box(0.0, table_width, 0.0, table_length);

  cc.add_constraint(couch);
  cc.add_constraint(coffee_table);
  cc.add_constraint(table);

  cc.set_bounding_area(0.0, room_width, 0.0, room_length);

  cc.solve();

  cc.print_solution();

}
```

There are two differences between this last test program and the listing for file test.cp:

- include file loosePk.h is used instead of geomCol.h
- object `cc` is derived from class `loose_packed_geom_collection` instead of `geometric_constraint_collection`

In the following example program, I define the room dimensions and the sizes of three pieces of furniture. I create a new `loose_packed_geom_collection` object `cc` and add the three furniture objects to it. The `loose_packed_geom_collection` class member functions `solve` and `print_solution` are called to find and print a solution, as seen in the following listing.

```
Use loose packed geometric constraint class to place furniture
Room width: 12, room height: 20

Best solution found:

Parameters:  best_index= 11, best_error= 0.02498

   Name: couch

      x_min, x_max: 0.431419, 3.931421
      y_min, y_max: 0.611037, 10.411059

   Name: coffee_table

      x_min, x_max: 8.233673, 10.433657
      y_min, y_max: 13.706219, 19.706202

   Name: table

      x_min, x_max: 6.441621, 11.441631
      y_min, y_max: 0.188717, 7.188726
```

Figure 3.4 shows the arrangement of objects produced by this test program.

The second listing in this section substitutes a `tight_packed_geom_collection` object for a `geometric_constraint_collection`. Using the same test data as the test program in Sec. 3.5, the following listing (file testb.cp in the directory named ch3 on the software disk) places constraint objects as close together as possible without overlapping.

```
// File: testB.cp
//
// Description: Test the tight packing geometric
//              constraint collection class

#include "tightPk.h"

const float room_width = 12.0;
const float room_length= 20.0;

const float couch_width = 3.5;
const float couch_length= 9.8;
```

```
const float coffee_table_width = 2.2;
const float coffee_table_length=6.0;

const float table_width = 5.0;
const float table_length= 7.0;

void main()
{
  cerr << "Use tight packing geometric constraint class"
       << " to place furniture\n";

  tight_packed_geom_collection cc;

  geometric_constraint couch("couch");
  couch.set_bounding_box(0.0, couch_width, 0.0, couch_length);

  geometric_constraint coffee_table("coffee_table");
  coffee_table.set_bounding_box(0.0, coffee_table_width,
                                0.0, coffee_table_length);

  geometric_constraint table("table");
  table.set_bounding_box(0.0, table_width, 0.0, table_length);

  cc.add_constraint(couch);
  cc.add_constraint(coffee_table);
  cc.add_constraint(table);

  cc.set_bounding_area(0.0, room_width, 0.0, room_length);

  cc.solve();

  cc.print_solution();

}
```

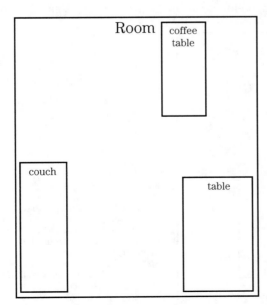

Figure 3.4 The `loose_packed_geom_collection` class arranges contained objects so that they do not overlap and tries to place them as far as possible from each other. The parameter `MAX_DEPTH` used in the function `geometric_constraint_collection::solve_by_relaxation()` determines how well the objects are arranged.

There are two differences between this last test program and the listing for file testA.cp:

- include file tightPk.h used instead of loosePk.h
- object cc is derived from class `tight_packed_geom_collection` instead of `loose_packed_geom_collection`

The following listing shows an example run from the tight packing geometric constraint test program.

```
Use tight packing geometric constraint class to place furniture
Room width: 12, room height: 20

Best solution found:

Parameters:  best_index= 106, best_error= 8.485004e-05

   Name: couch

      x_min, x_max: 0.429737, 3.929739
      y_min, y_max: 1.391093, 11.19106

   Name: coffee_table

      x_min, x_max: 4.035068, 6.235046
      y_min, y_max: 1.33581, 7.335766

   Name: table

      x_min, x_max: 6.271574, 11.271612
      y_min, y_max: 1.161635, 8.161602
```

Figure 3.5 shows the arrangement of objects produced by this test program.

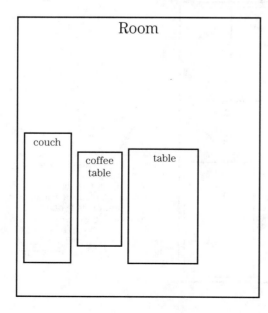

Figure 3.5 The `tight_packed_geom_collection` class arranges contained objects so that they do not overlap and tries to place them as close together as possible. The parameter MAX_DEPTH used in the function `geometric_constraint_collection::solve_by_relaxation()` determines how well the objects are arranged.

Chapter

4

Application Example: Capital Investment Planning For Small Businesses

The C++ constraint classes designed and developed in Chapter 2 can also be extended through subclassing to solve constraint problems for planning capital equipment purchases. To do so, I create a new subclass of constraint objects that are linked directly to other objects; all linked objects are allocated as a group. I create a new subclass of a constraint collection that attempts to allocate a subset of the objects it contains in order to maximize a utility function. The example program developed in this chapter will apportion a fixed capital equipment budget over a set of proposed capital equipment purchases, some of which may be linked to others (e.g., I only plan to purchase Apple printers when I purchase Macintosh computers, and I only purchase a walnut credenza if I purchase the matching walnut desk).

4.1 Extending the C++ Constraint Classes

Figure 4.1 shows the new constraint classes linked_constraint_collection, investment_constraint_collection, linked_constraint, and financial_ constraint being added to the constraint library developed in Chapter 2.

Instances of the class linked_constraint have a member variable that indicates whether the object has been allocated, as well as a list of pointers to other linked_constraint objects. The member function check_all_links_allo cated returns FALSE if any of the linked objects (including itself) is not marked as allocated, and TRUE if all linked objects are allocated.

Instances of the class linked_constraint_collection have interesting behavior: this class is derived from class constraint_collection, which maintains pointers to all the constraint objects that are contained in the collection. A linked_

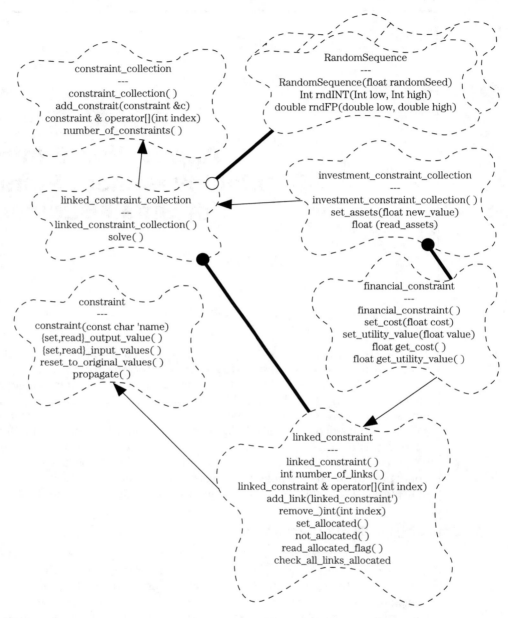

Figure 4.1 Add the following classes to those developed in Chapter 2: `linked_constraint_collection`, `investment_constraint_collection`, `linked_constraint`, and `investment_constraint`.

`constraint_collection` object provides a public member function `solve`, which returns FALSE if no contained objects or their linked objects are allocated, and TRUE if all contained objects and their linked objects are allocated.

The class `linked_constraint_collection` is not defined as an abstract base class because there are practical applications of this class, with no additional behavior required. However, in this chapter, I subclass `linked_constraint_collection` to create class `investment_constraint_collection`, which contains objects of a new class `financial_constraint` (as seen in Figure 4.1, this class is derived from class `linked_constraint`). Instances of class `financial_constraint` have private member variables for storing the cost and value of the object (the value often being a subjective measure!).

In summary, the new classes defined in Figure 4.1 make it possible to create a set of financial constraint objects and set links among some of these objects so that they either are or aren't allocated as a group. Each of these objects is assigned a cost and a utility value. When you put these `financial_constraint` objects into an `investment_constraint_collection`, you can use the `solve` behavior (member function) of that collection class to allocate, based on a fixed amount of available capital, the set of `financial_constraint` objects that maximizes the summed utility value for the collection.

Protected versus private member variables in a class

When you design your classes for any object-oriented language that supports the encapsulation of internal data, it is correct style to prevent direct public access of internal data. Here is an example of bad style:

```
class bad_class {
 public:
    bad_class();
    ~bad_class();
    float value; // public access violates principle of encapsulation
};

main()
{
    bad_class b;
    b.value = 1.0; // direct access to internal data
}
```

The following is the correct style:

```
class good_class {
 public:
    good_class();
    ~good_class();
    void set_value(float val) { value = val; }
    float get_value() { return value; }
 private:                 // P R I V A T E !!
    float value;
};

main()
{
    good_class g;
    g.set_value(1.0);
}
```

This is fine, and elementary, but when do I want to plan ahead and make private data protected? In good_class, I declare the member variable value to be private. If I then derive a new class new_good_class from good_class, the new member functions in this new class will not have access to that data. Sometimes this is the effect I want, but I often want derived classes to have access to private data, so I declare data to be protected instead of private. For example:

```
class base_class {
 public:
    base_class();
   ~good_class();
    void set_value(float val) { value = val; }
    float get_value() { return value; }
 protected:     // NOTE: protected instead of private
    float value;
};


class derived_class : public base_class {
 public:
    derived_class();
   ~derived_class();

      // NOTE: the following would be illegal if "value" were defined
      //       as private in base_class:

      float dummy_calc() { return 2.0 * value; } };

main()
{
    derived_class d;
    d.set_value(1.0);   // LEGAL for both protected and private value
       float x = d.dummy_calc();
}
```

When I first prototyped class financial_constraint, I defined the member variables cost and value to be protected, since I expected this class to be subclassed—I wanted to provide easy access directly to these member variables in derived classes. However, this was a mistake, since derived classes can use the member functions get_cost, set_cost, get_utility_value, and set_utility_value to access the private member variables. I like to think of derived classes adding a new layer to base classes, but with the derived class member functions using only the public interface to the base class. Figure 4.2 shows an illustration of this principle.

4.2 C++ Interface for the Linked Constraint Classes

The following listing shows the C++ interface for the class linked_constraint.

```
// File: linkedCn.h
//
// Description: This file contains the C++ interface for the class
//              linked_constraint, and is derived from class constraint.
```

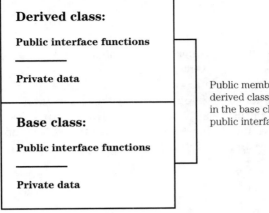

Public member functions in the derived class access private data in the base class only through the public interface of the base class

Figure 4.2 I prefer to access private data in base classes through the public interface of the base class. For some applications, I use protected base class member variables for more efficient access in time-critical software.

```
//
//
// This software may be used without restriction in compiled form.
//
// This source code may not be redistributed without permission.
//
#ifndef linkedCn_h
#define linkedCn_h

#include "constrn.h"

#include <iostream.h>

#include <math.h>

const int LINKED_TYPE = 4227;

const int LINKED_MAX_GRID = 64;

const int MAX_LINKED = 8; // maximum number of linked constraints

class linked_constraint : public constraint {
 public:
  linked_constraint(const char *my_name = "no_name");
  int number_of_links() { return num_links; }
  linked_constraint & operator[](int index);
  void add_link(linked_constraint & lc);
  void remove_link(int index);
  void set_allocated() { allocated_flag = 1; }
  void not_allocated() { allocated_flag = 0; }
  int read_allocated_flag() { return allocated_flag; }
  // utility that returns 1 if all links are allocated:
  int check_all_links_allocated();

private:
  int num_links;
  linked_constraint * links[MAX_LINKED];
  int allocated_flag;
```

```
};

#endif
```

The constant MAX_LINKED sets the maximum number of links to other linked_ constraint objects. This class is derived from class constraint, and adds the private member data for storing pointers to other linked linked_constraint objects. The public member function check_all_links_allocated provides the behavior of checking each of the num_links linked linked_constraint objects. It returns TRUE if all of these linked objects are allocated, otherwise returning FALSE.

The following listing shows the C++ interface for the class linked_constraint_ collection.

```
// File: linkCol.h
//
// Description: This file contains the C++ interface for the class
//              linked_constraint_collection, and is derived from
//              class constraint_collection.
//
//
// This software may be used without restriction in compiled form.
// This source code may not be redistributed without permission.
//
#ifndef linkCol_h
#define linkCol_h

#include "linkedCn.h"
#include "cnstrCol.h"


class linked_constraint_collection : public constraint_collection {
 public:
   linked_constraint_collection();
  ~linked_constraint_collection();

   // The solve() function here only checks for broken
   // link constraints.  That is, if any of the allocated
   // objects in this collection have linked objects that are
   // not allocated, then solve returns FALSE; if all linked
   // objects of all allocated members are also allocated,
   // then solve() returns TRUE.  Subclasses of this class
   // will probably call:
   //
   //       linked_constraint_collection::solve()
   //
   // and check the return value before doing anything else.

   virtual int solve();

};


#endif
```

The class linked_constraint_collection is derived from constraint_ collection, and adds the public behavior in member function solve, which checks for broken link constraints. Member function `solve` returns FALSE if any `linked_constraint` object in the collection has any links to unallocated objects, and returns TRUE if all link constraints are satisfied.

4.3 C++ Implementation of the Linked Constraint Classes

The following listing shows the C++ implementation for the class `linked_constraint`.

```
// File: linkedCn.cp
//
// Description: This file contains the C++ implementation for
//              class linked_constraint.
//
//
// This software may be used without restriction in compiled form.
// This source code may not be redistributed without permission.
//
#include "linkedCn.h"

//
//          Class constructor: linked_constraint
//

linked_constraint::linked_constraint(const char *my_name)
          : constraint(my_name)
{
#ifdef DEBUG
   cerr << "entering derived class 'linked_constraint' constructor: "
        << my_name << "\n";
#endif
  num_links = 0;
}


//
//          operator[]
//
//          This operator allows elements contained in
//          this collection to be referenced as if this
//          collection were an array.
//

linked_constraint &  linked_constraint::operator[](int index)
{
#ifndef FAST
   if (index < 0 || index > (MAX_LINKED - 1))
   {
      cerr <<  "linked_constraint::operator[]("
           << index << ") is illegal.  MAX_LINKED="
           << MAX_LINKED << "\n";
      exit(1);
   }
#endif
  return *links[index];
}


//
//          Member function: add_link
//
//          This function links a linked_constraint
```

```
//            instance (or an instance of any derived
//            class) to this object.
//

void linked_constraint::add_link(linked_constraint & lc)
{
#ifndef FAST
  if (num_links > (MAX_LINKED - 1))
    {
      cerr <<  "linked_constraint::add_link(): too many links"
           << ", MAX_LINKED=" << MAX_LINKED << "\n";
      exit(1);
    }
#endif
  links[num_links++] = &lc;
}


//
//            Member function: remove_link
//
//            This function removes a link to
//            another linked_constraint instance
//
void linked_constraint::remove_link(int index)
{
#ifndef FAST
  if (num_links < 0 || index >= num_links)
    {
      cerr <<  "linked_constraint::remove_link("
           << index << ") is illegal. num_links="
           << num_links << "\n";
      exit(1);
    }
#endif
  for (int i=index + 1; i<num_links; i++)
    links[i - 1] = links[i];
  num_links--;
}


//
//            Member function: check_all_links_allocated
//
//            This utility function returns TRUE if all
//            linked_constraint objects linked to this object
//            are allocated.
//

int linked_constraint::check_all_links_allocated()
{
  for (int i=0; i<num_links; i++)
    if (links[i]->read_allocated_flag() == FALSE)
      return FALSE;
  return TRUE;
}
```

The constructor for class linked_constraint simply calls the constructor for its base class constraint, and sets the member variable num_links to zero. The operator[] function is defined to enable easy access to the linked constraints.

Using operator[]

In collection classes, it makes sense to define `operator[]` to enable access to objects contained in the collection. Class `linked_object` is not a collection class, but it does contain a vector of pointers to other instances of class `linked_object`. It is important that the meaning of `operator[]` be clear to people who use the C++ classes that you design. In the case of `linked_object`, the class name strongly suggests that instances of the class are linked to other instances of the same class. For example:

```
linked_object PC("pc_clone");
linked_object tape_drive("tape_drive");
linked_object monitor("color monitor");

PC.add_link(tape_drive);
PC.add_link(monitor);

for (int i=0; i<PC.number_of_links(); i++)
{
        cerr << "object linked to " << PC.name << ": "
            << PC[i].name << "\n";       // use of operator[]
}
```

The class `linked_constraint` member function `add_link` adds a pointer to another instance of the `linked_constraint` class to the private vector of pointers to other `linked_constraint` objects. The member function `remove_link` removes a link at a specified index from the private vector links.

Each `linked_constraint` object contains a member data flag that indicates if the object is allocated. The meaning of "is allocated" is determined by the application that uses the class. When I designed this class, I anticipated that I would want to be able to easily check whether all `linked_constraint` objects linked to a given `linked_constraint` object had their `allocated` flag set to a value of TRUE. (The constant TRUE is set to 1 and the constant FALSE is set to 0 in the file constrn.h.) The `linked_constraint` member function `check_all_links_allocated` uses the private data vector links to find all linked objects. If any linked object has its `allocated` flag set to FALSE, then `check_all_links_allocated` returns FALSE; otherwise it returns TRUE.

The following listing of linkCol.cp shows the implementation of the class `linked_constraint_collection`.

```
// File: linkCol.cp
//
// Description: This file contains the C++ implementation of the
//              class linked_constraint_collection.
//
// This software may be used without restriction in compiled form. This
// source code can not be redistributed without permission.
//
#include "linkCol.h"
//
```

```
//              Class constructor: linked_constraint_collection
//
linked_constraint_collection::linked_constraint_collection()
        : constraint_collection()
{
}
//
//              Class destructor: linked_constraint_collection
//
linked_constraint_collection::~linked_constraint_collection()
{
}
//              Member function: solve
//
//              Note: The member function solve for this class
//                    will typically be called by derived classes
//                    to check that all necessary links are
//                    satisfied.

int linked_constraint_collection::solve()
{   int ret_val = 0;
    for (int nr=0; nr<get_num_constraints(); nr++)
    {
        constraint *gc = class_constraints[nr];
        if (gc->my_type() >= LINKED_TYPE)
        {
            linked_constraint *lc = (linked_constraint *)gc;
            if (lc->read_allocated_flag())
            {
                ret_val = 1;
                for (int i=0; i<lc->number_of_links(); i++)
                {
                    if ((*lc)[i].read_allocated_flag() == 0)
                        return 0;
                }
            }
        }
    }
    return ret_val;
}
```

The linked_constraint_collection collector only calls its base class constructor. The member function solve checks for broken link constraints.

4.4 Capital Investment Planner

As shown in Figure 4.1, I derived class financial_constraint from linked_
constraint (shown in Sec. 4.3), and class investment_constraint_collection
from linked_constraint_collection (also shown in Sec. 4.3). In this section I
show the interface to these derived financial planning classes (Sec. 4.4.1) and their
implementation (Sec. 4.4.2).

I derive class financial_constraint from class linked_constraint by
adding member data values to store cost and value parameters. I derive class
investment_constraint_collection from class linked_constraint_
collection by adding the following behavior and data:

- private member data to store total financial assets to spend

- private member data allocation_flags, which is used for constraint satisfaction calculations

- public member function `solve`, which tries to maximize the summed value of all purchased objects subject to the total expendable assets constraint and the linked object constraints

4.4.1 Interface to the C++ financial planning classes

The following listing shows the interface for the class `financial_constraint`.

```
// File: finance.h
//
// Description: This file contains the C++ interface for the class
//              financial_constraint, and is derived from class
//              linked_constraint.
//
// This software may be used without restriction in compiled form.
// This source code may not be redistributed without permission.
//
#ifndef finance_h
#define finance_h

#include "linkedCn.h"

#include <iostream.h>

#include <math.h>

const int FINANCIAL_TYPE = LINKED_TYPE + 1;

class financial_constraint : public linked_constraint {
 public:
   financial_constraint(const char *my_name = "no_name",
                        float the_cost = 0.0, float the_value = 0.0);
   float propagate();

   float get_cost() { return cost; }
   void  set_cost(float the_cost) { cost = the_cost; }
   float get_utility_value() { return value; }
   void  set_utility_value(float the_value) { value = the_value; }
   virtual int my_type()
   {
     return FINANCIAL_TYPE;
   }

    private:  // see notes in section 4.1 concerning private vs. protected
     float cost;
     float value;

};

#endif
```

This class is derived from `linked_constraint`. It adds private data for storing floating-point values for the cost of an object and its utility value (which can simply be entered as the cost, or can be a subjective estimate of the real value of the object). Here is an example showing the creation and linking of two financial_constraint objects:

```
financial_constraint Mac("Macintosh Centris 660AV", 2050.0, 2500.0);
financial_constraint monitor("Macintosh color 15-inch monitor", 600.0, 600.0);
```

```
// Only buy a Macintosh monitor if we buy the Macintosh:
   monitor.add_link(Mac);

// Only buy a Macintosh if we buy the Macintosh monitor:
   Mac.add_link(monitor);
```

In this example, I set up links so that I will not buy a Macintosh unless I also buy a monitor, and I will not buy a monitor unless I also buy a Macintosh. Sometimes I only want a one-way link; for example, I may only want to buy an Apple printer if I also buy a Macintosh, but I may buy a Macintosh and not a printer.

The following listing shows the interface for the class `investment_constraint_collection`.

```
// File: investCl.h
//
// Description: This file contains the C++ interface for the class
//              investment_constraint_collection, and is derived from
//              class constraint_collection.
//
//
// This software may be used without restriction in compiled form.
// This source code may not be redistributed without permission.
//
#ifndef investCl_h
#define investCl_h

#include "finance.h"
#include "linkCol.h"

const MAX_TRIALS = 200;

class investment_constraint_collection
        : public linked_constraint_collection
{
 public:
   investment_constraint_collection(float initial_assets = 0.0);
  ~investment_constraint_collection();
   int print_solution(); // returns TRUE if there is a solution

   virtual int solve();
 private:
   float assets;
   unsigned char allocation_flags[MAX_NODES][MAX_TRIALS];
   void set_to_trial(int index);
   int solution_found;
   int best_solution_index;
   void set_assets(float new_value) { assets = new_value; }
   float read_assets() { return assets; }
};

#endif
```

The class `investment_constraint_collection` is derived from class `linked_constraint_collection`. It adds private data for storing total cash assets available for purchases, and `allocation_flags` for constraint satisfaction calculations. The private member function `set_to_trial` is a utility used for setting the allocation flags in all `linked_constraint` (or `financial_constraint`) objects in the collection based on a trial index and the private array `allocation_flags`. The public member function solve attempts to satisfy link constraints and find the best set of purchase decisions meeting the constraint on the total expendable cash assets. Member function solve returns FALSE if it is unable to find a solution, and TRUE if a solution was found. If a solution is found, the allocation flags on each linked_constraint (or financial_constraint) object in the collection are set. After a solution is found, the member function read_allocated_flag can be used for each object in the collection to see if that object should be purchased.

4.4.2 Implementation of the C++ financial planning classes

The following listing shows the implementation of the class financial_constraint.

```
// File: finance.cp
//
// Description: C++ implementation of the class financial_constraint
//
//
// This software may be used without restriction in compiled form.
// This source code may not be redistributed without permission.
//

#include "finance.h"

//
//          Class constructor: financial_constraint
//

financial_constraint::financial_constraint(const char *my_name,
                                           float the_cost,
                                           float the_value)
          : linked_constraint(my_name)
{
#ifdef DEBUG
  cerr << "entering derived class 'financial_constraint'"
       << " constructor: " << my_name << "\n";
#endif
  cost = the_cost;
  value = the_value;
}

//
//          Return the (cost - value) if this node
//          is allocated as being purchased
//

float financial_constraint::propagate()
{
  if (my_container == NULL)
  {
    cerr << "NULL my_container pointer in linked_constraint"
         << "::propagate\n";
    exit(1);
  }

  //
  // Note: for financial constraints, we do not use local
  // propagation, just relaxation (letting the solve method
  // in the appropriate container collection class do the real
```

```
        // work).  We are in relaxation mode:
        //

        float ret_val = 0.0;

        if (read_allocated_flag())
        {
          ret_val = value - cost;
        }

        return ret_val;
}
```

The following listing shows the implementation of the class `investment_con straint_collection`.

```
// File: investCl.cp
//
// Description: This file contains the C++ implementation of the
//              class investment_constraint_collection.
//
//
// This software may be used without restriction in compiled form. //
// This source code may not be redistributed without permission.
//
#include "investCl.h"

//
//           Class constructor: investment_constraint_collection
//

investment_constraint_collection::investment_constraint_collection(
                                                        float money)
                 : linked_constraint_collection()
{
    assets = money;
    solution_found = FALSE;
}

//
//           Class destructor: investment_constraint_collection
//

investment_constraint_collection::~investment_constraint_collection()
{
}

//
//           Member function: set_to_trial
//
//           Note: member function solve sets up a series of trial
//                 purchase (allocation) values.  This function sets
//                 the allocation flags of all contained objects
//                 to trial set number 'index'.
//
void investment_constraint_collection::set_to_trial(int index)
{
#ifndef FAST
    if (index < 0 || index >= MAX_TRIALS) {
        cerr << "investment_constraint_collection::set_to_trial("
             << index << ") illegal. MAX_TRIAL=" << MAX_TRIALS << "\n";
        exit(1);
```

```
        }
#endif
    for (int i=0; i<get_num_constraints(); i++)
    {
        constraint *gc = class_constraints[i];
        if (gc->my_type() >= LINKED_TYPE)
        {
            financial_constraint *lc = (financial_constraint *)gc;
            if (allocation_flags[i][index] != 0)
                lc->set_allocated();
            else
                lc->not_allocated();
        }
    }
}

//
//          Member function: solve
//
//          Attempt to satisfy all link and cost constraints
//          while maximizing the value for a given budget.
//

int investment_constraint_collection::solve()
{
  float best_value = -9999.9;

  float temp_sum_cost, temp_sum_value;
  for (int i=0; i<MAX_NODES; i++)
  {
    for (int j=0; j<MAX_TRIALS; j++)
    {
        int iflag = 0;
        if (random_sequence->rndINT(0,10) > 6)
            iflag = 1;
        allocation_flags[i][j] = iflag;
    }
  }

  cerr << "\nTotal assets to spend: $" << read_assets() << "\n\n";

  for (int j=0; j<MAX_TRIALS; j++)
  {
      set_to_trial(j);

      if (linked_constraint_collection::solve() != 0)
      {
#ifdef DEBUG
          cerr << "Found a possible solution (link conditions satisfied)"
               << " at index " << j << "\n";
#endif
          temp_sum_cost = temp_sum_value = 0;

          for (int i=0; i<get_num_constraints(); i++)
          {
              constraint *gc = class_constraints[i];
              if (gc->my_type() == FINANCIAL_TYPE)
              {
                  financial_constraint *lc = (financial_constraint *)gc;
                  if (allocation_flags[i][j] != 0)
                  {
#ifdef DEBUG
                      cerr << lc->name << ", cost="
```

```
                                          << lc->get_cost() << ", utility="
                                          << lc->get_utility_value() << "\n";

                          for (int m=0; m<lc->number_of_links(); m++)
                          {
                              if ((*lc)[m].read_allocated_flag() == 0)
                                  cerr << (*lc)[m].name
                                          << " not allocated (error)\n";
                              else
                                  cerr << (*lc)[m].name << " allocated (OK)\n";

                          }
#endif
                          temp_sum_cost  += lc->.get_cost();
                          temp_sum_value += lc->get_utility_value();
                      }
                  }
              }

#ifdef DEBUG
          cerr << "sum cost=" << temp_sum_cost << "\n";
#endif
          if (temp_sum_cost <= read_assets())
          {
#ifdef DEBUG
              cerr << "   ** ** within budget\n\n";
#endif
              if (best_value < temp_sum_value)
              {
                  best_solution_index = j;
                  best_value = temp_sum_value;
              }
          }

      }
  }

  solution_found = (best_solution_index != -1);
  return solution_found;
}

//          Member function: print_solution
//
//          Print out the solution, if any, found by member
//          function solve.

int investment_constraint_collection::print_solution()
{
    if (solution_found != FALSE)
    {
      set_to_trial(best_solution_index);

      cerr << "\n\nBest solution at index: "
            << best_solution_index << "\n\n";

      for (int i=0; i<get_num_constraints(); i++)
      {
          constraint *gc = class_constraints[i];
          financial_constraint *lc = (financial_constraint *)gc;
          if (allocation_flags[i][best_solution_index] != 0)
          {
              cerr << lc->name << ", cost=""
                  << lc->get_cost() << ", utility="
                  << lc->get_utility_value() << "\n";
```

```
                for (int m=0; m<lc->number_of_links(); m++)
                {
                    if ((*lc)[m].read_allocated_flag() == 0)
                        cerr << "  required: " << (*lc)[m].name
                                << " not allocated (error)\n";
                    else
                        cerr << "  required: " << (*lc)[m].name
                                << " allocated (OK)\n";
                }


            }
        }
    }
    return solution_found;
}
```

4.5 Using the Financial Planning Classes for Planning Capital Equipment Purchases

The following example program listing defines the costs and link attributes of several pieces of equipment. An instance of the investment_constraint_collection class is used to plan purchases of these objects given a fixed amount of capital.

```
// File test.cp
//
// Description: Simple test of the financial modeling classes.
//              This example is meant as a guide to the notation
//              rather than a real example.  See the file 'bigtest.cp'
//              for a more interesting problem.  Here we solve:
//
//                  Total budget:                   $3400
//
//                  Possible purchases:
//
//                      Macintosh Centris 660AV:        $2050
//                      Macintosh color 15-inch monitor:  $600
//                      LaserWriter NT printer:         $1500
//
//                  Constraints:
//
//                      only buy a Macintosh monitor if we buy the Macintosh
//                      only buy a Macintosh if we buy the Macintosh monitor
//                      only buy a Macintosh printer if we buy the Macintosh


#include "linkedcn.h"
#include "finance.h"
#include "investCl.h"



void main()
{

    financial_constraint f1("Macintosh Centris 660AV", 2050.0, 2500.0);
    financial_constraint f2("Macintosh color 15-inch monitor", 600.0, 600.0);
    financial_constraint f3("LaserWriter NT printer", 1500.0, 1700.0);

    f2.add_link(f1);  // only buy a Macintosh monitor if we buy the Macintosh
```

```
f1.add_link(f2);   // only buy a Macintosh if we buy the Macintosh monitor
f3.add_link(f1);   // only buy a Macintosh printer if we buy the Macintosh

investment_constraint_collection ic(3400.0);
ic.add_constraint(f1);
ic.add_constraint(f2);
ic.add_constraint(f3);

if (ic.solve() != 0)
{
   cerr << "\nsolve() found a solution.\n";
   ic.print_solution();
} else
{
   cerr << "\nNo solution found.\n";
}
}
```

The following listing shows the output from this program (compiled without
DEBUG set):

```
Total assets to spend: $3400


solve() found a solution.


Best solution at index: 13

Macintosh Centris 660AV, cost=2050, utility=2500
   required: Macintosh color 15-inch monitor allocated (OK)
Macintosh color 15-inch monitor, cost=600, utility=600
   required: Macintosh Centris 660AV allocated (OK)
```

This simple example program shows the syntax for setting up a capital equipment
purchase plan. The constructor for class `financial_constraint` takes three arguments: the name of the object, the purchase price, and an estimate of the value.
Usually, we set the value of an object to its purchase price; these values can be ad-
justed, however, in order to prejudice the purchase decision on selected objects.
   The following listing shows a more complete example.

```
// File bigtest.cp
//
// Description: Test of the financial modeling classes.
//
//              Plan to buy capital equipment based on these constraints:
//
//                   Total budget:                      $9500
//
//                   Possible purchases:
//
//                       Macintosh Centris 660AV:        $2050
//                       Macintosh color 15-inch monitor: $600
//                       LaserWriter NT printer:         $1500
//                       IBM PC 486 clone                $1500
//                       Generic laser printer           $1200
//                       Portable 486 machine (B&W)      $2100
//                       Portable 486 machine (color)    $3800
```

```
//
//                    Constraints:
//
//                        only buy a Macintosh monitor if we buy the Macintosh
//                        only buy a Macintosh if we buy the Macintosh monitor
//                        only buy a Macintosh printer if we buy the Macintosh
//
//              Note: In a practical application of this program with
//                    hundreds of proposed capital equipment purchases,
//                    start with the "value" of each item equal to its
//                    cost. If some items are deemed more important,
//                    increase their "value" to be slightly higher
//                    than their cost, and rerun this program.
//
//


#include "linkedcn.h"
#include "finance.h"
#include "investCl.h"

void main()
{
  financial_constraint

      MacCentris("Macintosh Centris 660AV", 2050.0, 2500.0),
      MacMonitor("Macintosh color 15-inch monitor", 600.0, 600.0),
      NTprinter("LaserWriter NT printer", 1500.0, 1700.0);

  // Only buy a Macintosh monitor if we buy the Macintosh:
  MacMonitor.add_link(MacCentris);
  // Only buy a Macintosh if we buy the Macintosh monitor:
  MacCentris.add_link(MacMonitor);
  // Only buy a Macintosh printer if we buy the Macintosh:
  NTprinter.add_link(MacCentris);

  financial_constraint

      PC486("486 PC", 1500.0, 1500.0),
      GenericLaser("Generic laser printer", 1200.0, 1200.0),
      Portable486_1("Portable 486 (B&W)", 2100.0, 2100.0),
      Portable486_2("Portable 486 (B&W)", 2100.0, 2100.0),
      Portable486_3("Portable 486 (B&W)", 2100.0, 2100.0),
      PortableColor486("Portable 486 (color)", 3800.0, 2900.0);

  investment_constraint_collection ic(9500.0);

  ic.add_constraint(MacCentris);
  ic.add_constraint(MacMonitor);
  ic.add_constraint(NTprinter);
  ic.add_constraint(PC486);
  ic.add_constraint(GenericLaser);
  ic.add_constraint(Portable486_1);
  ic.add_constraint(Portable486_2);
  ic.add_constraint(Portable486_3);
  ic.add_constraint(PortableColor486);

  if (ic.solve() != 0)
  {
    cerr << "\nsolve() found a solution.\n";
    ic.print_solution();
  } else
  {
    cerr << "\nNo solution found.\n";
```

```
  }
}
```

The following listing shows the output from this program (compiled without DEBUG set):

```
Total assets to spend: $9500

solve() found a solution.

Best solution at index: 177

Macintosh Centris 660AV, cost=2050, utility=2500
   required: Macintosh color 15-inch monitor allocated (OK)
Macintosh color 15-inch monitor, cost=600, utility=600
   required: Macintosh Centris 660AV allocated (OK)
LaserWriter NT printer, cost=1500, utility=1700
   required: Macintosh Centris 660AV allocated (OK)
486 PC, cost=1500, utility=1500
Portable 486 (B&W), cost=2100, utility=2100
```

Genetic Algorithms

5

Analysis for the
Genetic Algorithm Classes

Genetic algorithms form a good basis for solving some optimization, search, and learning problems. Genetic algorithms are particularly appropriate for quickly finding good solutions to problems, but not necessarily the best solution for a given problem specification. Human experts are not typically judged by how close to optimal their decisions are, but by how quickly they can make decisions, and how well their decisions compare to decisions made by other experts under similar circumstances (Goldberg, 1989).

For purposes of analysis, I examine the simulation of genetically based objects that mutate and have a fitness for survival based on a numerical fitness function. This analysis yields an unstructured understanding of genetic algorithms. For the design process in the next chapter, I create class hierarchies that abstract the implementation details and yield a set of genetic algorithm classes with a clean public interface.

5.1 Definition of Terms

Genetic algorithms are inspired by the study of genetics; they borrow terms from genetics and simulate the adaptive behavior of biological systems. The smallest data item that encodes information is the gene. Problem information is encoded by a sequence of genes; this ordered collection is the chromosome. The position of a specific gene in a chromosome is the locus. We allow the information in genes to mutate, that is, the information can occasionally change randomly. Mutations usually involve relatively small changes. Another type of variation is the crossover, in which a random locus is chosen where two genes are split; the two genes then exchange the portion occurring after the locus. The formula specifying how well a given chromosome solves the formulated problem is called the fitness. Fitness is represented by a function of one argument—a chromosome—that returns a fitness value. The population is a set of chromosomes with initial random values that are used to solve a problem. The number of generations is the number of times the population is varied and the fitness values calculated in solving a problem. A complete problem description with directions for mutations, crossovers, and the number of generations is called an experiment.

5.2 A Simple Example: Location of New Restaurants

In this section, I propose a trivial problem and discuss how to formulate that problem using genetic algorithms.

Problem description

Suppose I want to place new fast food restaurants along Main Street. I have three optimization constraints: I want to spread the restaurants out so that no two are close together, I want them to be close to the new mall entrance, and I would prefer to build three new restaurants.

My first task is to represent this problem in genetic terms. Main Street is 16 blocks long. I choose one-bit genes; each gene has a value of zero if there isn't a new restaurant on this block, and one if there is. Thus, our locus addresses genes from zero to fifteen, which correspond to blocks one through sixteen on Main Street.

I need to define a fitness function that

- maximizes the average distance between all new restaurants;
- awards a fitness bonus when three genes are equal to one (I would prefer to have three new restaurants);
- minimizes the closest distance between a new restaurant and the entrance to the new mall.

To solve this problem, I perform the following tasks:

- choose an initial random population size (I use 10 chromosomes)
- Set up the initial random population of chromosomes, randomly fill the 10 chromosomes, setting about 30% of the bits to one. For each of 100 generations:
- find the best four out of 10 chromosomes;
- vary the four selected chromosomes to get a new population of 10;
- select the "most fit" chromosome from the population of any generation as a "good" solution to the problem.

To appreciate how simple it is to express this problem as a genetic algorithm problem, I use the class library developed in Chapter 6 to solve this problem with a 28 line program.

The following listing (of the test.cp file in the genetic directory on the software disk) shows the solution to this problem using the C++ class library listed in Chapter 6.

```
// File: test.cp
//
// Description: This file solves the problem posed in Chapter 5:
//
//      • chromosomes are 16 genes long
//      • each chromosome codes the existence of a new restaurant (1 = yes)
//        on the block number == to locus (gene) index
//      • fitness = maximize distance between restaurants,
//                    bonus for number of restaurants == 3,
//                    minimize distance to mall (at block/gene index 10)
//
//

#include "genexp.h"

float chromosome::fitness()
{
    // Bonus for # of restaurants == 3:
    int i, count = number_of_on_bits();
    float value = 10000.0;
    int delta = count - 3;
    if (delta < 0)  delta = -delta;
    value -= 300.0 * delta;

    // reduce fitness if restaurants are on adjacent blocks:
    int my_size = size();

    for (i=0; i<my_size-2; i++)
    {
        if ((*this)[i])
        {
            if ((*this)[i+1])  value -= 200; // on adjacent blocks
            if ((*this)[i+2])  value -= 100; // 2 blocks away
        }
    }

    float distance = 0.0;
    for (i=0; i<my_size - 2; i++)
        if ((*this)[i])
            for (int j=i+1; j < my_size - 1; j++)
                if ((*this)[j])
                    distance += 10*(j - i);

     value += distance;

    // Special bonus if restaurant is on the same block as the new Mall:
    if ((*this)[10])  value += 800;

    return value;
}

void main()
{   char ch;
    genetic_experiment ge(16, 20, 25.0); // chrom size, pop size, mut rate
    for (int i=0; i<12; i++)
    {
#ifdef DEBUG
        cerr << "\nIteration " << i << "\n";
#endif
        ge.solve();
#ifdef DEBUG
        cerr << "** current best fitness ="
                << ge.current_best_fitness() << "\n";
#endif
```

```
    }
    cerr << "\n\n16 blocks:\n\n";
    chromosome *best = ge.current_best_chromosome();
    for (i=0; i<16; i++) {
        cerr << "block #" << i << ", restaurant flag: "
            << (*best)[i] << "\n";
    }
}
```

This listing shows how simple it is to solve optimization problems when you can express the problem with a bit-vector data structure (in this case representing each block on a street as a single bit, with a one bit indicating a new restaurant location) and can express the "fitness" of a chromosome as a simple calculation. The example in Chapter 7 will be much more complex than this simple example.

The following listing shows the output of this program (compiled without DEBUG set):

```
constructor for genetic_experiment:

    chromosome size = 16
    population_size = 20

16 blocks:

block #0, restaurant flag: 0
block #1, restaurant flag: 1
block #2, restaurant flag: 0
block #3, restaurant flag: 0
block #4, restaurant flag: 0
block #5, restaurant flag: 0
block #6, restaurant flag: 0
block #7, restaurant flag: 0
block #8, restaurant flag: 0
block #9, restaurant flag: 0
block #10, restaurant flag: 1
block #11, restaurant flag: 0
block #12, restaurant flag: 0
block #13, restaurant flag: 0
block #14, restaurant flag: 1
block #15, restaurant flag: 0
```

In this program output, notice that the planning goals are met: a new restaurant was placed on block 10, and the three new restaurants were not placed near each other.

This simple example shows the syntax for expressing a constraint problem as a fitness function for a genetic algorithm program. In the next chapter, I develop the C++ class libraries to support this simple example, and I develop an application in Chapter 7 for site planning.

5.3 Overview of Genetic Algorithm Software

Genetic algorithm simulation software will contain gene, chromosome, and experiment control objects.

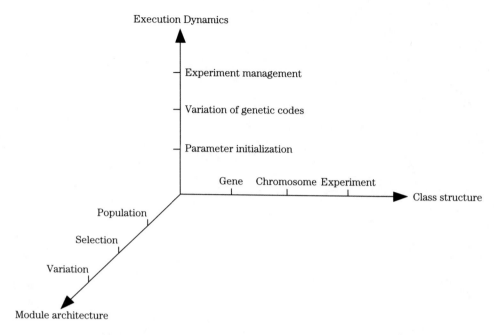

Figure 5.1 Organization of software to support experiments with genetic algorithms. This graph has three dimensions: class structure, module architecture, and program execution dynamics. The class structure will be expressed in the class diagram shown in Chapter 6. The module architecture is reflected in the organization of classes into physical source files.

Design and Implementation of the C++ Genetic Algorithm Classes

I discussed typical genetic algorithm application problems in Chapter 5 and analyzed the requirements of a C++ genetic algorithm class library. In this chapter, I design and implement a set of C++ classes that provide the data structures and behavior of the following types of genetic algorithm objects: experiment collection, chromosomes, and genes.

In the analysis in Chapter 5, I decomposed the problem of simulating genetic objects. In this chapter, the goal is to create class hierarchies for simulating populations of genetic objects, abstracting the implementation details from the clients of these genetic C++ classes.

6.1 Overview of the C++ Class Structure

I will design four classes for experimenting with genetic algorithms: `bit_vector`, `gene_sequence`, `chromosome`, and `genetic_experiment`. In genetic algorithm simulations, individual genes in a chromosome are usually represented by a single bit. Since `bit_vector` objects are useful for other applications besides genetic algorithms, I designed a separate `bit_vector` class that supports setting and testing individual bits in a compact vector of bits. I derive the class `gene_sequence` from class `bit_vector`. I then derive class `chromosome` from class `gene_sequence`, adding behavior for mutation and genetic crossovers. I could have implemented these three classes as a single class, but I did not for two reasons:

- class `bit_vector` will be useful in other applications;
- class `gene_sequence` might be modified in the future to allow data formats other than single bits to represent genes.

I believe that it is better to design derived classes that add new layers of behavior (or functionality) to their base classes. This division into multiple derived classes makes it much easier to modify programs.

The class `genetic_experiment` controls a set of chromosomes during an experiment, including finding a single chromosome with the largest fitness value. These classes are diagrammed in Figure 6.1.

6.2 C++ Interface Definition

The following C++ class headers are listed in this section:

- `bit_vector`
- `gene_sequence`
- `chromosome`
- `genetic_experiment`

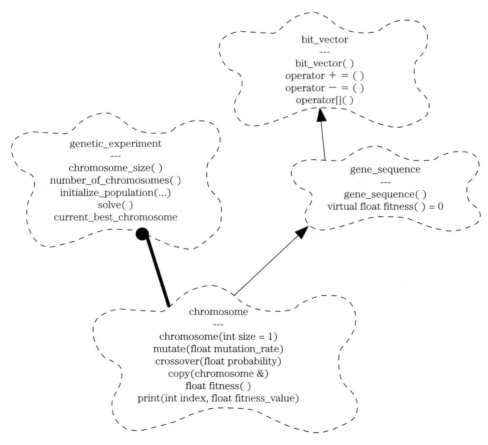

Figure 6.1 Class diagram for the genetic algorithm experiment class library.

The following listing shows the interface for the `bit_vector` class.

```
// File: bit_vec.h
//
// Description: This file contains the C++ interface for the
//              class bit_vector.
//
//
#ifndef bit_vec_h
#define bit_vec_h

#include <iostream.h>

const BITS_PER_INT = 8 * sizeof(unsigned int);

class bit_vector {
 public:
    bit_vector(int num_bits = 1);
   ~bit_vector();
    unsigned int operator[](int bit_index);
    int number_of_on_bits();
    void operator+=(int bit_to_turn_on);
    void operator-=(int bit_to_turn_off);
    int operator==(bit_vector &other);
    void set_to_zero();
    void set_to_one();
    int size()
    {
      return number_of_bits;
    }

 protected:
    unsigned int * data;
    int number_of_bits;
    int number_of_ints;

};
#endif
```

The following listing shows the C++ interface for the `gene_sequence` class.

```
// File: gene.h
//
// Description: This file contains the C++ interface for the
//              gene_sequence class.
//
// This software may be used without restriction in compiled form.
// This source code may not be redistributed without permission.
//
#ifndef gene_h
#define gene_h

#include "bit_vect.h"

class gene_sequence : public bit_vector
{
 public:
    gene_sequence(int size = 1);
   ~gene_sequence();
    virtual float fitness() = 0;  // abstract base class
};

#endif
```

The following listing shows the C++ interface for the chromosome class.

```
// File: chromo.h
//
// Description: This file contains the C++ interface for the
//              chromosome class.  Note that we use public
//              inheritance from the gene_sequence class instead of
//              a "uses" class relationship so that the gene_sequence
//              operators are directly accessible.  Also, a chromosome
//              "is a kind of" gene_sequence, with extra added behavior.
//
//
// This software may be used without restriction in compiled form.
// This source code may not be redistributed without permission.
//
#ifndef chromo_h
#define chromo_h

#include "randseq.h"
#include "gene.h"
#include <stdlib.h>

class chromosome : public gene_sequence {
 public:
    chromosome(int size = 1);
    chromosome(chromosome & chromosome_to_copy);
   ~chromosome();
    void mutate(float mutation_rate);
    void copy(chromosome & chromosome_to_copy);
    // perform "in place" without creating a new chromosome:
    void crossover(chromosome & other_chromosome);
    // Define the following member function in your application:
    float fitness();
    void print(int index = 0, float fitness = -999.9);
 private:
    RandomSequence random_seq;
};

#endif
```

The member function copy is used to make an exact copy of a chromosome. The member function mutate randomly mutates bits in a chromosome. The member function crossover takes another chromosome as its argument; a chromosome and its partner swap genetic material at a randomly chosen bit index.

The following listing shows the C++ interface for the genetic_experiment class.

```
// File: genexp.h
//
// Description: This file contains the C++ interface
//              for class genetic_experiment. Instances
//              of this class control the management of
//              a set of trial learning iterations.
//
//              NOTE: An application program will define at
//                    least one subclass of chromosome that
//                    has a "fitness" function defined for
//                    the application.  The genetic_experiment
//                    class is subclassed to provide a special
//                    allocate_chromosome function that can
//                    allocate any subclass of chromosome and
//                    return a pointer to it.
```

```
//
//
// This software may be used without restriction in compiled form.
// This source code may not be redistributed without permission.
//
#ifndef genexp_h
#define genexp_h

#include "chromo.h"

class genetic_experiment {
 public:
    genetic_experiment(int chrom_size = -1,
                       int population_size = -1,
                       float mutation_rate = 25.0,    // 25 %
                       float crossover_probability = 0.3);
   ~genetic_experiment();
    int chromosome_size() { return size_of_chromosome; }
    int number_of_chromosomes();
    virtual void initialize_population();
    void solve();
    float current_best_fitness();
    chromosome * const current_best_chromosome();
 private:
    chromosome **chromosomes;
    int size_of_population;
    int size_of_chromosome;
    int current_best_chromosome_index;
    float mut_rate;
    float cross_prob;
    float *fitnesses;
    void sort_by_fitness();
    RandomSequence randoms;
};

#endif
```

6.3 C++ Implementation

The following listing shows the implementation of the bit_vector class (found in the util directory on the software disk).

```
// File: bit_vec.cp
//
// Description: This file contains the C++ implementation for the
//              class bit_vector.
//
//
// This software may be used without restriction in compiled form.
// This source code may not be redistributed without permission.
//
#include "bit_vect.h"

//
//          Class constructor: bit_vector
//

bit_vector::bit_vector(int num_bits)
{
```

```
        number_of_ints = (num_bits + (BITS_PER_INT - 1)) / BITS_PER_INT;
        number_of_bits = num_bits;
        data = new unsigned int[number_of_ints];
        set_to_zero();
    }


    //
    //          Class destructor: bit_vector
    //

    bit_vector::~bit_vector()
    {
        delete [] data;
    }


    //
    //          operator[]
    //
    //          Note: this operator[] can only be used
    //                on the RHS (right side of the = sign).
    //
    //                Do not try this:
    //
    //                    bit_vector b(10);
    //                    b[2] = 1;
    //
    //                Instead do this:
    //
    //                    bit_vector b(10);
    //                    b += 1;  // peculiar syntax for setting bit 1
    //
    unsigned int bit_vector::operator[](int bit_index)
    {
        return ((data[bit_index / BITS_PER_INT] &
                (1 << (bit_index % BITS_PER_INT)))
            != 0);
    }


    //
    //          Member function: number_of_on_bits
    //

    int bit_vector::number_of_on_bits()
    {
        int ret_val = 0;
        for (int i=0; i<number_of_bits; i++)
            if (data[i / BITS_PER_INT] & (1 << (i % BITS_PER_INT)))
                ret_val++;
        return ret_val;
    }


    //
    //          operator+=
    //
    //          to use operator+= to turn on bits.  For an example:
    //
    //              bit_vector b(10);
    //              b += 0;  // strange, but this turns on the first bit!
    //

    extern "C" { void exit(int); };

    void bit_vector::operator+=(int bit_to_turn_on)
    {
```

```
#ifndef FAST
    if (bit_to_turn_on < 0 || bit_to_turn_on >= number_of_bits)
    {
        cerr << "error: bit_to_turn_on=" << bit_to_turn_on < "\n";
        exit(1);
    }
#endif
    data[bit_to_turn_on / BITS_PER_INT] |=     (1 <<
 (bit_to_turn_on % BITS_PER_INT));
}


//
//          operator-=
//
//          Use operator-= to turn off bits.  For an example:
//
//              bit_vector b(10);
//              b -= 5;  // strange, but this turns off the sixth bit!
//

void bit_vector::operator-=(int bit_to_turn_off)
{
#ifndef FAST
    if (bit_to_turn_off < 0 || bit_to_turn_off >= number_of_bits)
    {
        cerr << "error: bit_to_turn_off=" << bit_to_turn_off << "\n";
        exit(1);
    }
#endif
    data[bit_to_turn_off / BITS_PER_INT] &=
        (~(1 << (bit_to_turn_off % BITS_PER_INT)));
}


//
//          operator==
//
//          Use operator== to test for equality between 2 bit_vectors
//

int bit_vector::operator==(bit_vector &other)
{
#ifndef FAST
    int size_other = other.size();
    if (number_of_bits != size_other)
    {
        cerr << "bit_vector::operator== size mismatch\n";
        exit(1);
    }
#endif
    for (int i=0; i<number_of_bits; i++)
    {
        if ((*this)[i] != other[i])
        {
            return 0;
        }
    }
    return 1;
}


//
//          Member function: set_to_zero
//
//          Clears all bits to zero
//
```

```
void bit_vector::set_to_zero()
{
    for (int i=0; i<number_of_ints; i++)
        data[i] = 0;
}

//
//          Member function: set_to_one
//
//          Sets all bits to one
//

void bit_vector::set_to_one()
{
    for (int i=0; i<number_of_ints; i++)
        data[i] = 1;
}
```

The following listing contains the implementation for the gene_sequence class
(source file gene.cp is located in the genetic directory on the software disk).

```
// File: gene.cp
//
// Description: This file contains the C++ implementation for the
//              gene_sequence class.
//
//
// This software may be used without restriction in compiled form.
// This source code may not be redistributed without permission.
//
#include "gene.h"

//
//      Note: currently, a gene_sequence is simply
//            a clone of the bit_vector class.  It
//            makes sense to rename a bit_vector to
//            gene_sequence for this application.  Also,
//            application-specific behavior can be added
//            to the gene_sequence class without altering
//            the underlying bit_vector utility class.
//

gene_sequence::gene_sequence(int size) : bit_vector(size)
{
}

gene_sequence::~gene_sequence()
{
}
```

The following listing shows the implementation of the chromosome class:

```
// File: chromo.cp
//
// Description: This file contains the C++ implementation for
//              the chromosome class.
//
//
// This software may be used without restriction in compiled form.
// This source code may not be redistributed without permission.
```

```
//

#include "chromo.h"
#include "randseq.h"

//
//              Class constructor # 1: chromosome
//

chromosome::chromosome(int size) : gene_sequence(size)
{

}


//
//              Class constructor #2: chromosome
//

chromosome::chromosome(chromosome & chromosome_to_copy)
     : gene_sequence(chromosome_to_copy.size())
{
  int size = chromosome_to_copy.size();
  for (int i=0; i<size; i++)
      if (chromosome_to_copy[i])
          (*this) += i;
      else
          (*this) -= i;
}

//
//              Class destructor: chromosome
//

chromosome::~chromosome()
{
}
//
//              Member function: copy
//
//              Copies another chromosome's data into
//              this chromosome.
//

void chromosome::copy(chromosome & chromosome_to_copy)
{
  int size = chromosome_to_copy.size();
  set_to_zero();
  for (int i=0; i<size; i++)
      if (chromosome_to_copy[i])
          (*this) += i;
      else
          (*this) -= i;
}

//
//              Member function: mutate
//
//              This function can randomly mutate the genes
//              in this chromosome.
//

void chromosome::mutate(float mutation_rate) // measured in percent
{
```

```
      if (random_seq.rndFP(0.0, 100.0) < mutation_rate)
      {
          int mutation_location = random_seq.rndINT(0, size() - 1);
#ifdef DEBUG
          cerr << "mutation location = " << mutation_location << "\n";
#endif
          if ( (*this)[mutation_location] )
              (*this) -= mutation_location;
          else
              (*this) += mutation_location;
      }
}


//
//          Member function: crossover
//
//          This function randomly chooses a gene index,
//          swaps genetic material with 'other_chromosome'.
//

// perform "in place" without creating a new chromosome
void chromosome::crossover(chromosome &other_chromosome)
{
      // Swap genes between this chromosome
      // and other_chromosome at a randomly calculated
      // crossover position:

      int my_size = size();
      int crossover_location = random_seq.rndINT(1, my_size / 2 - 1);
      if (my_size != other_chromosome.size())
      {
          cerr << "chromosome::crossover(): size mis-match: "
              << my_size << ", " << other_chromosome.size() << "\n";
          exit(1);
      }

#ifdef DEBUG
      cerr < "crossover location = " << crossover_location << "\n";
#endif

      for (int i=0; i<crossover_location; i++)
      {
          int save = (*this)[i];
          if (other_chromosome[i])
              (*this) += i;
          else
              (*this) -= i;
          if (save)
              other_chromosome += i;
          else
              other_chromosome -= i;
      }
}

//
//
//          Member function: print
//

void chromosome::print(int index, float fitness)
{
      cerr << "chromosome " << index << " : ";
      int my_size = size();
      for (int i=0; i<my_size; i++) {
```

```
        if ((*this)[i])
            cerr << "1 ";
        else
            cerr << "0 ";
    }
    cerr << "fitness = " << fitness << "\n";
}
```

The following listing shows the implementation of the genetic_experiment class.

```
// File: genexp.cp
//
// Description: This file contains the C++ interface
//              for class genetic_experiment. Instances
//              of this class control the management of
//              a set of trial learning iterations.
//
//
// This software may be used without restriction in compiled form.
// This source code may not be redistributed without permission.
//

#include "genexp.h"

//
//          Class constructor: genetic_experiment
//
//          (see class discussion in Chapter 6)
//

genetic_experiment::genetic_experiment(int chrom_size,
                                       int population_size,
                                       float mutation_rate,
                                       float crossover_probability)
{
    cerr << "constructor for genetic_experiment:\n\n";
    cerr << "   chromosome size = " << chrom_size << "\n";
    cerr << "   population_size = " << population_size << "\n";
    if (population_size < 0 || chrom_size < 0)
    {
        cerr << "genetic_experiment::genetic_experiment() illegal\n";
        exit(1);
    }
    if (population_size < 8)
    {
        cerr << "illegal: population size should be >= 8\n";
        exit(1);
    }
    size_of_population = population_size;
    size_of_chromosome = chrom_size;
    mut_rate = mutation_rate;
    cross_prob = crossover_probability;
    chromosomes = new chromosome * [population_size];
    for (int i=0; i<population_size; i++)
        chromosomes[i] = new chromosome(size_of_chromosome);

    fitnesses = new float[population_size];
    initialize_population();
    sort_by_fitness();
}

//
```

```
//          Class destructor: genetic_experiment
//
genetic_experiment::~genetic_experiment()
{
    delete [] chromosomes;
    delete [] fitnesses;
}


//
//          Member function: number_of_chromosomes
//
//          Return the number of trial chromosomes
//          in the genetic experiment.
//

int genetic_experiment::number_of_chromosomes()
{
    return size_of_population;
}

//
//          Member function: initialize_population
//

void genetic_experiment::initialize_population()
{
    for (int i=0; i<size_of_population; i++)
    {
        for (int j=0; j<size_of_chromosome / 2; j++)
        {
            int index = randoms.rndINT(0,size_of_chromosome-1);
            (*chromosomes[i]) += index;
        }
        fitnesses[i] = chromosomes[i]->fitness();
    }
}
void genetic_experiment::sort_by_fitness()
{
    // sort by fitness, best fitness in chromosomes[0]:
    float x;
    chromosome * c;

    for (int i=0; i<size_of_population; i++)
    {
        for (int j=(size_of_population - 2); j>=i; j—)
        {
            if (fitnesses[j] < fitnesses[j+1])
            {
               x = fitnesses[j];
               c = chromosomes[j];
               fitnesses[j]     = fitnesses[j+1];
               chromosomes[j]   = chromosomes[j+1];
               fitnesses[j+1]   = x;
               chromosomes[j+1] = c;
            }
        }
    }
}


//
//          Member function: solve
//
//          Use genetic algorithms to find a trial
//          chromosome that has a high fitness value, as
```

```
//            calculated by chromosome::fitness().
//

void genetic_experiment::solve()
{
    // start by copying the best half of the population
    // into the worst half of the population:
    int i = 0, j;

    for (j=size_of_population-3; j<size_of_population; j++)
    {
        chromosomes[j]->copy(*chromosomes[i++]);
    }

    // do the crossovers:
    i = 0;
    for (j=size_of_population-5; j<size_of_population-1; j++)
    {
        chromosomes[j]->crossover(*chromosomes[i++]);
    }

    // do the mutations (do not mutate the best chromosome):
    for (j=1; j<size_of_population; j++)
    {
        chromosomes[j] -> mutate(mut_rate);
    }
    for (i=0; i<size_of_population; i++) {
        fitnesses[i] = chromosomes[i]->fitness();
    }

    sort_by_fitness();
#ifdef DEBUG
    for (j=0; j<size_of_population; j++)   {
        chromosomes[j]->print(j, fitnesses[j]);
    }
#endif
}

//
//
//          Member function: current_best_fitness
//
//          Return the current best fitness from
//          the chromosome population in this
//          genetic experiment.
//

float genetic_experiment::current_best_fitness()
{
    return fitnesses[0];
}

//
//
//          Member function: current_best_chromosome
//
//          Return the current best chromosome from
//          the chromosome population in this
//          genetic experiment.
//
chromosome * const genetic_experiment::current_best_chromosome()
{
    return chromosomes[0];
}
```

The example program listed in Chapter 5 demonstrates the use of these classes. That example optimized the location of new restaurants along a single street. The example was easy to implement because a street could be trivially represented by the bit vectors used to model chromosomes. In Chapter 7, you will see a more interesting example that optimizes the location of new restaurants in a city represented by a two-dimensional grid.

Application Example: Optimize the Locations of Fast-Food Restaurants in a City

We often find that if we can abstract a good representation of a problem, obtaining a solution is easy. But abstraction is not always simple. As problem solvers, we normally have two modes of thinking. Most of the time we react to our environment and act (and to a limited degree also think!) reflexively, based on prior experience. However, most of the good, creative work we do is a product of a reflective mode of thinking, in which we sort through facts dealing with the problem at hand and reorganize what we know into new mental data structures. As good problem solvers, we examine the problem at hand, eliminate unnecessary detail by making abstractions, and create a relatively simple representation of the problem. In our minds, the simple representation becomes the problem, and enables us to deal effectively with complexity.

In this chapter, I want to optimize the placement of a chain of fast-food restaurants in a city. This is a complex problem dealing with site location selection, building costs, competing restaurants, and population density.

7.1 Initial Representation

In attempting to abstract a simple yet meaningful representation, I will do what is common in science: make use of what we are able to measure and calculate, and ignore everything else!

The first abstraction that I make is to treat the city streets as a uniform two-dimensional grid. Figure 7.1 illustrates this mapping ("rubber sheeting") of a real road network onto a regular grid.

As I attempt to abstract meaningful representations of the problem, it is useful to iteratively refine the design of the representation in the same way that good soft-

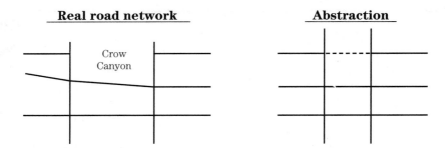

Figure 7.1 The first abstraction that we make is to ignore curved roads and map all roads to a two-dimensional grid.

ware developers iterate over the development steps of analysis, design and implementation. (Actually, iteratively refining the abstraction of a good representation of a problem is one of the key steps in analysis.)

It is worthwhile writing down preliminary representations of a problem even though the representation will evolve. As a practical matter, it is not a good idea to try to determine the best representation for a complex problem at one time. "Sleep on it," try a small experimental program using your representation, and you will get new ideas for improving your representation, thus improving your analysis, design and implementation.

Since you are going to use your C++ genetic algorithm class library to solve this problem, you will need to map a two-dimensional street array into a one-dimensional chromosome array (a bit vector). This is actually very easy to do, as Figure 7.2 shows for the hypothetical town of SmallVille.

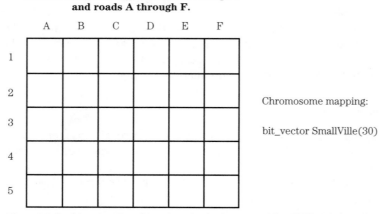

Figure 7.2 In this representation, a location in the town of SmallVille is specified by road (run West to East) and street (run North to South) indices. Thus, any block location in SmallVille can be represented by a bit in a bit vector of length 30.

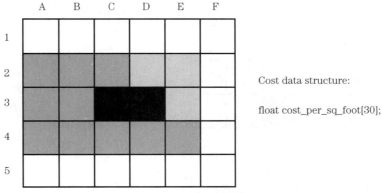

Relative building costs. Darker shading indicates higher building costs

Cost data structure:

float cost_per_sq_foot[30];

Figure 7.3 The estimated cost per square foot can be represented by a one-dimensional array. It is also useful (for human problem solvers!) to have a graphic display of relative building costs overlaid on a map of the city.

The representation shown in Figure 7.2 is certainly simple, and it is useful enough to use for a while. I also want to represent building costs based on the area of town (this will mostly be a function of the price of property). Figure 7.3 shows a simple representation for building costs in different areas of town.

The problem representation shown in Figures 7.2 through 7.5 makes a simplifying assumption that building sites are uniformly available across the town of SmallVille.

7.2 Improved Representation

Real data for a city would include a list of possible building sites, including the estimated purchase price for each parcel of property. I can improve my initial problem

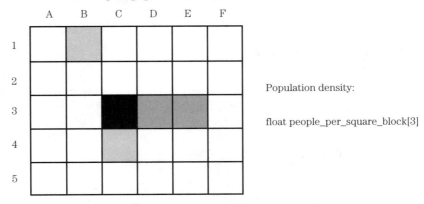

Relative Population Density. Darker shading indicates a higher population density.

Population density:

float people_per_square_block[3]

Figure 7.4 Population density in the town of SmallVille.

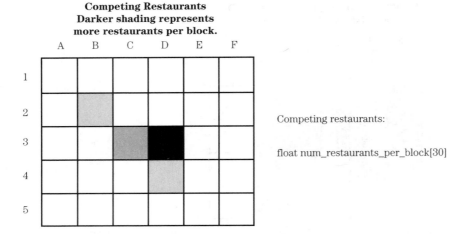

Figure 7.5 Density of competing restaurants in the town of SmallVille.

representation shown in Sec. 7.1 by mapping the list of possible sites onto a chromosome. We might use the following data to represent the problem:

```
const int NUM_SITES = 10;
const int NUM_STREETS = 5; // run West to East
const int NUM_ROADS = 6; // run North to South

chromosome site_selection_candidate(NUM_SITES);
float population_density[NUM_ROADS][NUM_STREETS];
float cost_per_sq_foot[NUM_ROADS][NUM_STREETS];
float competition_density[NUM_ROADS][NUM_STREETS];
```

I will need these data structures to calculate a fitness value for each proposed chromosome, that is, for each proposed site selection. For example, if gene numbers two, four, and seven are set to one (rather than zero), that means that the chromosome represents the selection of the second, fourth, and seventh sites as locations for the new restaurants.

7.3 Calculation of a Fitness Function

Figures 7.3, 7.4, and 7.5 show the relative building costs, population density, and density of competing restaurants in different parts of the town of SmallVille. In the example program listed in Sec. 7.4, I fill in the following data structures:

```
float population_density[NUM_ROADS][NUM_STREETS];
float cost_per_sq_foot[NUM_ROADS][NUM_STREETS];
float competition_density[NUM_ROADS][NUM_STREETS];
```

I determine the relative value of each trial chromosome by using the following equations (from the fitness function listed in Sec. 7.4):

```
value -= cost_per_sq_foot[road][street] * COST_FACTOR;
value -= competition_density[road][street]
            *  COMPETITION_FACTOR;
value += population_density[road][street]
            *  POPULATION_FACTOR;
```

The constants COST_FACTOR, COMPETITION_FACTOR, and POPULATION_FAC
TOR are defined near the beginning of the file test.cp listed in Sec. 7.4, and should be
changed to alter the weighting of the optimization criteria.

7.4 Implementation of the Restaurant Site Selection Program

The following listing shows the test program for this chapter.

```
// File: test.cp
//
// Description: This file solves the problem posed in Chapter 7:
//
//       • Town of SmallVille has a road system represented by
//         a two-dimensional grid of NUM_STREETS by NUM_ROADS
//         (see Figure 7.2)
//       • There are different building costs in different parts
//         of town (due mostly to different prices of land)
//         (see Figure 7.3)
//       • The population density varies (see Figure 7.4)
//       • The density of competing restaurants varies (see Figure 7.5)
//
//
// This software may be used without restriction in compiled form.
// This source code may not be redistributed without permission.
//

#include "genexp.h"

const int NUM_SITES = 10;
const int NUM_STREETS = 5; // run West to East
const int NUM_ROADS = 6; // run North to South

const int NUMBER_NEW_RESTAURANTS = 10;   // preferred number

const float COST_FACTOR = 2.0;
const float COMPETITION_FACTOR = 10.0;
const float POPULATION_FACTOR = 25.0;

const int POPULATION_SIZE = 20; // # genetic samples
const float MUTATION_RATE = 25.0;   // 25 %

chromosome site_selection_candidate(NUM_SITES);
float population_density[NUM_ROADS][NUM_STREETS];   // people per block
float cost_per_sq_foot[NUM_ROADS][NUM_STREETS];
float competition_density[NUM_ROADS][NUM_STREETS];

RandomSequence randomObject;

// Initialize the data structures for the town of SmallVille
// (see Figures 7.1 through 7.5 in the book):

static void initialize_SmallVille()
{
    // Initialize data structures with good defaults:
```

```
for (int road=0; road<NUM_ROADS; road++)
{
    for (int street=0; street<NUM_STREETS; street++)
    {
        population_density[road][street] =
                randomObject.rndFP(0.5, 5.0);
        cost_per_sq_foot[road][street] =
                randomObject.rndFP(50.0, 60.0);
        competition_density[road][street] =
                randomObject.rndFP(0.01, 0.1);   // low average
    }
}
// Override default values for specific areas of town:

// Building costs (see Figure 7.3):
cost_per_sq_foot[0][1] = 70.0;
cost_per_sq_foot[1][1] = 70.0;
cost_per_sq_foot[2][1] = 70.0;
cost_per_sq_foot[0][2] = 70.0;
cost_per_sq_foot[1][2] = 70.0;
cost_per_sq_foot[0][3] = 70.0;
cost_per_sq_foot[1][3] = 70.0;
cost_per_sq_foot[0][4] = 70.0;
cost_per_sq_foot[1][4] = 70.0;
cost_per_sq_foot[2][4] = 70.0;
cost_per_sq_foot[3][4] = 70.0;
cost_per_sq_foot[4][4] = 70.0;
cost_per_sq_foot[3][1] = 110.0;
cost_per_sq_foot[4][1] = 110.0;
cost_per_sq_foot[2][2] = 140.0;
cost_per_sq_foot[3][2] = 140.0;

// Population density (see Figure 7.4):
population_density[1][0] = 10.0;
population_density[2][4] = 10.0;
population_density[3][2] = 20.0;
population_density[4][2] = 20.0;
population_density[2][2] = 30.0;

// Competing restaurant density (see Figure 7.5):

competition_density[1][1] = 0.5;
competition_density[3][3] = 0.5;
competition_density[2][2] = 1.0;
competition_density[3][2] = 2.5;

}

float chromosome::fitness()
{
    // Bonus for # of restaurants == 3:
    int i, count = number_of_on_bits();

    // OPTIMIZATION: It is very important to minimize the amount
    //               of time required to calculate the fitness
    //               function. We only want chromosomes that have
    //               NUMBER_NEW_RESTAURANTS bits set, so we quickly
    //               return a small value if this is not the case:

    if ( count != NUMBER_NEW_RESTAURANTS)   return 0.0;

    float value = 10000.0;

    // reduce fitness if restaurants are on adjacent blocks:
    int my_size = size();
```

```cpp
    for (i=0; i<my_size; i++)
    {
        int bit_set =  (*this)[i];
        if (bit_set)
        {
            int road = i / NUM_STREETS;
            int street = i - (road * NUM_STREETS);

            value -= cost_per_sq_foot[road][street] * COST_FACTOR;
            value -= competition_density[road][street]
                        * COMPETITION_FACTOR;
            value += population_density[road][street]
                        * POPULATION_FACTOR;
        }
    }

    return value;
}


void main()
{
    initialize_SmallVille();
    int number_of_genes = NUM_STREETS * NUM_ROADS;
    genetic_experiment ge(number_of_genes,
                          POPULATION_SIZE, MUTATION_RATE);
    for (int i=0; i<500; i++)
    {
#ifdef DEBUG
        cerr << "\nIteration " << i << "\n";
#endif
        ge.solve();
#ifdef DEBUG
        cerr << "** current best fitness ="
            << ge.current_best_fitness() << "\n";
#endif
    }

    // For converting road indices into names:
    static char * road_names[] = {"A", "B", "C", "D", "E",
                                  "F", "G", "H", "I", "J",
                                  "K", "L", "M", "N", "O"};
    cerr << "\nSmallVille optimization parameters:\n\n";
    cerr << "  Cost factor        = " << COST_FACTOR << "\n";
    cerr << "  Competition factor = " << COMPETITION_FACTOR << "\n";
    cerr << "  Population factor  = " << POPULATION_FACTOR << "\n";
    cerr << "  Prefered number of new restaurants to build = "
        << NUMBER_NEW_RESTAURANTS << "\n\n";
    cerr << "Recommended sites:\n\n";

    chromosome *best = ge.current_best_chromosome();
    for (i=0; i<number_of_genes; i++)
    {
        int bit_set =  (*best)[i];
        if (bit_set)
        {
            int road = i / NUM_STREETS;
            int street = i - (road * NUM_STREETS);

            cerr << "  Site at road: " << road_names[road]
                << ", and street: " << street + 1 << "\n";
        }

    }
}
```

7.5 Example Output from the Restaurant Site Selection Program

The following listings show several outputs from the example program for various optimization parameters.

The following listing uses reasonable default values for the optimization factors, which take into account that the average population density values are about 5.0, the average cost per square foot for construction is about $60, and the average competition density is about 0.3 in the sample test program.

```
constructor for genetic_experiment:

   chromosome size = 30
   population_size = 20

SmallVille optimization parameters:

   Cost factor       = 2
   Competition factor = 10
   Population factor  = 25
   Preferred number of new restaurants to build = 10

Recommended sites:

   Site at road: B, and street: 1
   Site at road: C, and street: 2
   Site at road: C, and street: 4
   Site at road: D, and street: 4
   Site at road: D, and street: 5
   Site at road: E, and street: 1
   Site at road: E, and street: 3
   Site at road: E, and street: 4
   Site at road: F, and street: 2
   Site at road: F, and street: 5
```

The next listing shows the effect of increasing the population factor, so that we build in areas of highest population density.

```
constructor for genetic_experiment:

   chromosome size = 30
   population_size = 20

SmallVille optimization parameters:

   Cost factor       = 2
   Competition factor = 10
   Population factor  = 300
   Preferred number of new restaurants to build = 10

Recommended sites:

   Site at road: A, and street: 3
   Site at road: A, and street: 4
   Site at road: A, and street: 5
   Site at road: C, and street: 2
   Site at road: D, and street: 3
```

```
Site at road: E, and street: 1
Site at road: E, and street: 2
Site at road: F, and street: 1
Site at road: F, and street: 3
Site at road: F, and street: 5
```

The next listing shows the effect of increasing the competition factor, so that we build in areas of lowest competition density.

```
constructor for genetic_experiment:

   chromosome size = 30
   population_size = 20

SmallVille optimization parameters:

   Cost factor        = 2
   Competition factor = 110
   Population factor   = 25
   Preferred number of new restaurants to build = 10

Recommended sites:

   Site at road: A, and street: 1
   Site at road: A, and street: 4
   Site at road: B, and street: 1
   Site at road: B, and street: 4
   Site at road: C, and street: 4
   Site at road: D, and street: 5
   Site at road: E, and street: 2
   Site at road: E, and street: 5
   Site at road: F, and street: 4
   Site at road: F, and street: 5
```

Figure 7.6 The parameter NUMBER_OF_RESTAURANTS was set to 10 in the example program. This causes a preferred selection for chromosomes with 10 bits set. This graph shows the number of bits set per chromosome as a function of time. Note that the system learns to produce samples with close to the correct number of bits set through mutation and crossover.

7.6 Adaptive Learning

The genetic algorithm C++ classes developed in Chapter 6 learn by an optimized search through the parameter space for the problem being solved. It is interesting to note that the search itself is adaptive! The C++ classes start out by producing default chromosomes with about one third of their bits randomly set. Clearly, this default is often not appropriate to the optimization problem at hand. The genetic algorithm simulation implemented in C++ classes quickly learns to produce trial chromosomes with approximately the correct number of bits set. Figure 7.6 shows this interesting behavior.

Genetic algorithms allow for very efficient search of large parameter spaces. The sample problem in this chapter executes in about one second on a 486 PC clone.

Neural Networks

Analysis for the Neural Network Classes

Neural networks are now a standard technique for solving pattern-matching problems (Watson 1991; Watson 1993). They are appropriate for solving a wide range of such problems when a large body of training data is available.

In this chapter, I analyze the process of simulating neural networks. My goal is to lay out the implementation details, refining your understanding of the mechanics of neural network simulations. In the next chapter, I design C++ classes for neural network simulations that hide the implementation details revealed in this chapter.

8.1 Requirements for the C++ Neural Network Classes

Even though neural network simulation software is fairly simple to implement, I still want to encapsulate the data required for the simulation, the behavior for training the network, and the behavior needed to use trained networks for recognition tasks. As always, I want to make the external interface to the C++ classes simple to use.

Neural networks use two types of objects, which will be reflected in our class design:

data objects
- neurons
- neuron layers
- arrays of connection weights which interconnect adjacent neuron layers
- neural network (contains neuron layers and connection weights)

control objects
- neural trainer
- recall manager

A neuron is characterized by an activation energy. In my neural models, I will not design a C++ class for individual neurons. Instead, my most primitive C++ neural network object will be the neuron layer, which is a one-dimensional vector of floating-point activation energies (one for each neuron in the layer). There are two special neural layers in a neural network: the input layer and the output layer. The neurons in the input layer have their activations set by some agency external to the neural network. The neurons in the output layer make the activation energies available outside the network.

Even though I implement a neuron layer as a one-dimensional vector of activation values, you will shortly see (Figure 8.3) that the input to a neural network is often logically treated as a two-dimensional array of values.

The connection weights store the knowledge in a neural network; they will be implemented as a two-dimensional array. For example, if the input neuron layer contains three neurons, and the hidden neuron layer contains two neurons, then I use a two-dimensional array of size 3*2 to completely connect the activation energy of each input neuron to the input of each hidden layer neuron (see Figure 8.1).

In this book, I am going to use three- and four-layer neural networks. I define a three-layer neural network as containing

- a one-dimensional input neuron layer

- a two-dimensional array of connection weights connecting the input neural layer to the hidden neuron layer

5 Neurons in 2 Neuron Layers:

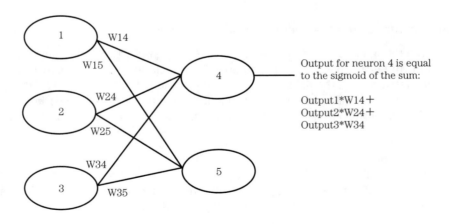

Output for neuron 4 is equal to the sigmoid of the sum:

Output1*W14+
Output2*W24+
Output3*W34

Neuron layer N   **Neuron layer N+1**

Figure 8.1 Output values of a neuron are a function of the output values of input neurons and the connection weight strengths which connect the neurons. Neural networks learn by adjusting the connection strength weights (W14 through W35 in the figure).

- a one-dimensional hidden neuron layer
- a two-dimensional array of connection weights connecting the hidden neuron layer to the output neuron layer
- a one-dimensional output neuron layer

Some neural network researchers call this a two-layer network (they do not count the input layer).

I define a four-layer neural network as containing

- a one-dimensional input neuron layer
- a two-dimensional array of connection weights connecting the input neural layer to the first hidden neuron layer
- a one-dimensional hidden neuron layer (first hidden layer)
- a two-dimensional array of connection weights connecting the first hidden neuron layer to the second hidden neuron layer
- a one-dimensional hidden neuron layer (second hidden layer)
- a two-dimensional array of connection weights connecting the second hidden neuron layer to the output neuron layer
- a one-dimensional output neuron layer

Some neural network researchers call this a three-layer network (they do not count the input layer).

I also want two classes of objects for controlling the behavior of neural networks: neural trainers and recall managers. A neural trainer object has the behavior of training (setting appropriate values of all connection weights) a neural network using a training data file (the format of this file will be presented in Sec. 10.3). A recall manager object facilitates using a previously trained neural network object for pattern recognition and control applications.

As you can see in Figure 8.1, the output activation of a given neuron is calculated by multiplying the output value of each input neuron by the connection weight value for the link between the input neuron and the current neuron. The sum of these products is "squashed" in value by a so-called sigmoid function. The derivative of this same sigmoid function is used in the learning equation for modifying connection strength weights. The sigmoid function and its derivative are shown in Figure 8.2.

The input neurons in a neural network are special: they receive their activation (or output) values from signals external to the neural network. The output neurons are also special: their output values are read outside the neural network and are typically interpreted to identify the present input pattern applied to the input neurons. A simple example (from Watson (1991)) will illustrate this process: recognizing handwritten characters. The input neurons of a neural network are arranged in a two-dimensional grid, as seen in Figure 8.3.

Neural networks learn to detect features in input data. As an example, in a handwriting recognition system, we might train the neural network to recognize the numbers zero through nine by writing each number twenty times, thus creating two

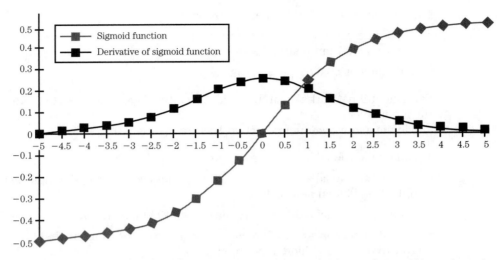

Figure 8.2 A sigmoid function is used to limit a neuron's output value for very large positive and negative values. The derivative of the sigmoid function will be used to implement the internal behavior of a neural network trainer object.

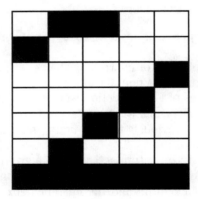

Figure 8.3 The 35 input neurons in a neural network are arranged in a 7×5 grid. A single handwritten character is mapped onto this grid. Where we have written, corresponding input neurons are given the maximum output value (+0.5) and where we have not written, corresponding input neurons are given the minimum output value (−0.5).

hundred individual training examples like the one in Figure 8.3. In the twenty examples of writing the number "2," each example will be slightly different from the others. By providing many training examples, the neural network generalizes the features of "2" that differentiate it from other numbers. The differences between the different samples of the number "2" become noise, which the neural network learns to ignore.

In practice, there are usually at least three layers of neurons: input, hidden, and output. The number of input neurons is determined by the number of system inputs. The number of output neurons is determined by the number of required outputs. It is often a good idea to encode output values with a small number of output neurons. For example, if the desired output of a neural network is to turn a switch on or off, then a single output neuron is used. If the network needs to choose among three al-

Three output neurons can be interpreted as
the three bits, and can thus encode the integers 0 through 7:

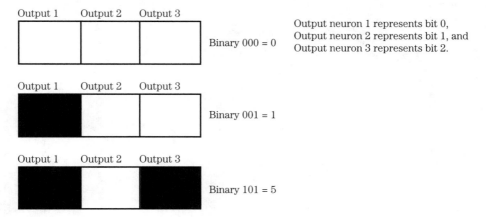

Output neuron 1 represents bit 0,
Output neuron 2 represents bit 1, and
Output neuron 3 represents bit 2.

Note that output neurons which are black, have a high activation energy and
are given a binary value of 1 and output neurons which are not black in these
three examples have a binary value of 0.

Figure 8.4   Three examples of using three output neurons to encode the values 0, 1, and 5.

ternatives, it is reasonable to use three separate output neurons, one for each output
state. However, if a network needs to indicate a decision among many possible outputs, it is better to encode the output value as a binary number. Figure 8.4 shows
how this is done.

8.2 Example Neural Network Applications

Neural networks are useful whenever you need to solve a pattern recognition problem and have training data available that contains many examples of both system inputs and outputs.

In Chapter 10, we train a neural network to help us make buy/no-buy decisions for
consumer goods. How well this network performs is a function of the training data
that we provide it.

In Chapter 11, we train a neural network to control simple, hypothetical factory
equipment. Again, the performance of this neural network will depend on the qual-
ity of training data.

Design and Implementation of the C++ Neural Network Classes

I analyzed the requirements of a C++ neural network class library and discussed typical neural network application problems in Chapter 8. In this chapter, I design and implement a set of C++ classes for providing the data structures and behavior of the following types of neural network objects: neuron layer (collection of neurons), neural data sets, connection weight sets, neural network trainer, and a neural network recall manager. The goal in this chapter is to abstract the implementation details identified in Chapter 8 into a set of C++ classes.

9.1 Overview of the C++ Class Structure

The first step in using a neural network is to train it using training data. A `neural_data` object contains ("has-a" class relationship) the `neuron_layer` and `connection_weights` data objects required to specify a neural network. A `neural_trainer` object manages the training of the neural network weights in a `neural_data` object. A `recall_manager` object uses a previously trained `neural_data` object to solve pattern-recognition problems.

The knowledge of learned patterns and behavior is stored in the connection weight values of a neural network. I have separated the two-dimensional connection weight array data into two separate classes: `connection_row` and `connection_weights`. By defining `operator[]` member functions for both classes, you can index a `connection_weight` object as:

```
connection_weight cw(input_size, hidden_size);
float val = cw[input_neuron_index][hidden_neuron_index];
```

Figure 9.1 shows the classes in the C++ neural network library. The class hierarchy is fairly simple, with no subclassing. You may want to subclass the `neural_trainer` class in your applicatons if you want to experiment with different neural network learning techniques.

Figure 9.1 Neural Network C++ class diagram. The class `neural_data` declares classes `neural_trainer` and `recall_manager` as friend classes.

9.2 C++ Interface Definition

The following C++ class headers are listed in this section:

data classes
- neuron layer
- connection_row
- connection_weight (contains a vector of connection_rows)
- neural_data (all data for a neural network)

control classes
- neural_trainer
- recall_manager

The following C++ include defines the interface for the neuron_layer class.

```
// File: nlayer.h
//
// Description: This file contains the C++ interface for the
//              neuron_layer class.
//
//
// This software may be used without restriction in compiled form.
// This source code may not be redistributed without permission.
//

#ifndef nlayer_h
#define nlayer_h

class neuron_layer {
 public:
    neuron_layer(int num_neurons);
    ~neuron_layer();
    int num_neurons();
    double & operator[](int index);
    void set_layer_values(double value);
 private:
    double *data;
    int number_of_neurons;
};
#endif
```

Since I do not have a separate class for individual neurons, the neuron_layer class is the most primitive neural network C++ object. The private data element data is a pointer to number_of_neurons double floating-point values. We define operator[] to provide access to the individual neuron activation energies in the neuron_layer. The class constructor will allocate storage for the activation energy values, and the class destructor frees the storage for the activation energy values.

The following C++ include defines the C++ interface for the connection_row class.

```
// File: con_row.h
//
// Description: This file contins the C++ interface for the
//              connection_row class.
//              A sequence of connection_row objects is used
//              to form a two-dimensional connection weight
//              array.  The advantage of using two classes is
//              that we can define operator[] for each class
//              to allow double indexing like: weight[i][j]
//
//
// This software may be used without restriction in compiled form.
// This source code may not be redistributed without permission.
//

#ifndef con_row_h
#define con_row_h

class connection_row {
 public:
    connection_row(int size = -1);
   ~connection_row();
    double & operator[](int index);
    int num_values();
 protected: // we will need to subclass in Chapter 12 with data access
    double *data;
    int number_of_values;
};

#endif
```

A connection_row object is simply a one-dimensional vector of double floating-point values. This class is used in the connection_weight class to provide two-dimensional array references with operator[] for two-dimensional arrays of connection weights.

The following C++ include defines the C++ interface for the connection_ weights class.

```
// File: weights.h
//
// Description: This file contains the C++ implementation for the
//              connection_weight class. This class contains a
//              sequence of connection_row objects to form a
//              two-dimensional array.
//
//
// This software may be used without restriction in compiled form.
// This source code may not be redistributed without permission.
//

#ifndef weights_h
#define weights_h

#include "con_row.h"

class connection_weights {
 public:
    connection_weights(int num_in, int num_out);
    connection_row & operator[](int from_row_index);
 private:
```

```
        connection_row ** rows;
        int num_from;   // number of input neurons
        int num_to;     // number of output neurons
};

#endif
```

The `connection_weight` class implements a two-dimensional array of connection weights for interconnecting `neuron_layer` objects. Note that with `operator[]` defined in both this class and the `connection_row` class, we provide the convenient two-dimensional array notation that we saw in Sec. 9.1.

The following C++ `include` defines the C++ interface for the `neural_data` class.

```
// File: ndata.h
//
// Description: This file contains the C++ interface for the
//              neural_data class.
//
//
// This software may be used without restriction in compiled form.
// This source code may not be redistributed without permission.
//

#ifndef ndata_h
#define ndata_h

#include "nlayer.h"
#include "weights.h"

class neural_data {

 friend recall_manager;
 friend neural_trainer;

 public:
    neural_data(int input_size, int hidden_size, int output_size);
    neural_data(int input_size, int hidden_1_size, int hidden_2_size, int output_size);
    neural_data(const char * file_name); // used by recall managers and neural_trainers:
    void propagate_activations();
    int save_to_disk(const char *file_name);
    int restore_from_disk(const char *file_name);
    void set_inputs(connection_row &new_inputs);
    void set_inputs(neuron_layer &new_inputs);
    void read_outputs(neuron_layer &output_values);
 private:
    int num_layers;
    int input_layer_size;
    int hidden_1_layer_size;
    int hidden_2_layer_size;   // not used for a four-layer network
    int output_layer_size;
    neuron_layer *inputs;
    neuron_layer *hidden_1;
    neuron_layer *hidden_2;   // not used for a four-layer network
    neuron_layer *outputs;
    connection_weights *weights_1;
    connection_weights *weights_2;
    connection_weights *weights_3;   // not used for a four-layer network
};

#endif
```

Instances of the `neural_data` class contain all data objects for implementing either a three- or four-layer neural network. These objects are made persistent by the `neural_trainer` and `recall_manager` objects by writing all data for a `neural_data` object to a disk file (we use the file extension ".net" in the example programs). Instances of the `neural_data` class have the following interesting behavior:

- they have three class constructors
- constructor for a new three-layer network
- constructor for a new four-layer network
- constructor that reads a ".net" network file, and reconstructs a previously trained `neural_data` object
- they can propagate activation energies from the input `neuron_layer` through to the output `neuron_layer` using interconnecting hidden `neuron_layers` and `connection_weights`
- they can save themselves to a ".net" data file
- they can restore themselves from a ".net" data file
- they can set the activation values of their input neurons (private data) with a supplied one-dimensional vector of `double` floating-point values
- they can provide the current output `neuron_layer` activation energy values

The following C++ `include` defines the C++ interface for the `neural_trainer` class.

```
// File: trainer.h
//
// Description: This file contain the C++ interface for the
//              class neural_trainer. An instance of this class
//              is used to create a trained 'neural_data' object,
//              which can be saved to disk as a persistent object
//              for later use. Note: the constructor for this class
//              does it all: reads the training data, trains the network,
//              saves the network to disk, and frees memory.
//
//
// This software may be used without restriction in compiled form.
// This source code may not be redistributed without permission.
//

#ifndef trainer_h
#define trainer_h

class neural_trainer {
 public:
    neural_trainer(const char *input_training_data_set_name,
                   const char *output_trained_neural_data_name);
    double final_training_error();
    ~neural_trainer();
 private:
};

#endif
```

The class constructor for the `neural_trainer` class has interesting behavior. The constructor has two required `const char *` arguments:

- the name of a training data file name
- the name of a file to use for saving a trained `neural_data` object

The class constructor automatically creates a new `neural_data` object, trains it with the supplied data, and then saves the `neural_data` object to the specified ".net" network data file. This automatic behavior is exactly what I want for most neural network applications. I create a training data file, and then create a persistent (through a ".net" network file) `neural_data` object that I can embed in my applications using a `recall_manager` object.

The following C++ `include` defines the C++ interface for the `recall_manager` class.

```
// File: recall.h
//
// Description: This file contains the C++ interface for
//              the recall_manager class.
//
//
// This software may be used without restriction in compiled form.
// This source code may not be redistributed without permission.
//

#ifndef recall_h
#define recall_h

#include "ndata.h"

class recall_manager {
 public:
    recall_manager(const char *neural_data_file);
   ~recall_manager();
    void calculate_outputs(neuron_layer &new_inputs);
    double operator[](int output_index);
 private:
    neuron_layer *outputs;
    neural_data  *data;
};

#endif
```

The constructor for the `recall_manager` class reads a ".net" data file, and creates as private data a `neuron_data` object that has been previously trained by a `neural_trainer` object. Instances of this class have two additional behaviors that allow `neural_data` objects to be easily embedded in applications:

- the `calculate_outputs` member function sets the input `neuron_layer` activation values, and propagates these values through all internal connection weights and neuron layers to the output `neuron_layer`
- the `operator[]` member function returns a specified output neuron activation value

9.3 C++ Implementation

The following listing contains the implementation for the `neuron_layer` class.

```
// File: nlayer.cp
//
// Description: This file contains the C++ implementation for
//              the neuron_layer class.
//
//
// This software may be used without restriction in compiled form.
// This source code may not be redistributed without permission.
//
#include "iostream.h"
#include "nlayer.h"
#include <stdlib.h>

//
//          Class constructor: neuron_layer
//

neuron_layer::neuron_layer(int num_neurons = -1)
{
    if (num_neurons == -1)
    {
        cerr << "neuron_layer::neuron_layer(" << num_neurons
            << "):  illegal, specify size of layer in "
            << "constructor\n";
        exit(1);

    }
    number_of_neurons = num_neurons;
    data = new double[num_neurons];
    if (data == (double *)NULL)
    {
        cerr << "neural_layer constructor cannot allocate data\n";
        exit(1);
    }
}


//
//          Class destructor: neuron_layer
//
neuron_layer::~neuron_layer()
{
    delete [] data;
}

//
//          Member function: num_neurons
//
//          Returns the number of neurons in this layer (slab).
//

int neuron_layer::num_neurons()
{
    return number_of_neurons;
}


//
//          operator[]
//
//          Allows referencing neurons in this layer as
```

```
//              if the layer were a simple array of neurons.
//

double & neuron_layer::operator[](int index)
{
    if (index < 0 || index >= number_of_neurons)
    {
        cerr << "illegal index: neuron_layer::operator[]\n";
        exit(1);
    }
    return (double &) data[index];
};

//
//          Member function: set_layer_values
//
//          Sets all neurons in this layer to a specified value.
//

void neuron_layer::set_layer_values(double value)
{
    for (int i=0; i<number_of_neurons; i++)
        data[i] = value;
}
```

The constructor for class neuron_layer has one required argument, the number of neurons in the layer. The constructor allocates storage for one activation energy value for each neuron in the layer. The class destructor frees this space.

The following listing contains the implementation for the connection_row class.

```
// File: con_row.cp
//
// Description: This file contains the C++ implementation for the
//              connection_row class.
//
//
// This software may be used without restriction in compiled form.
// This source code may not be redistributed without permission.
//
#include "con_row.h"
#include "iostream.h"
#include <stdlib.h>

//
//          Class constructor: connection_row
//

connection_row::connection_row(int num_neurons)
{
    if (num_neurons == -1)
    {
        cerr << "connection_row::connection_row(" << num_neurons
             << "):  illegal, specify size of layer in"
             << " constructor\n";
        exit(1);

    }
    number_of_values = num_neurons;
    data = new double[num_neurons];
    if (data == (double *)NULL)
    {
```

```
          cerr << "connection_row constructor cannot allocate data\n";
          exit(1);
      }
}

//
//          Class destructor: connection_row
//
connection_row::~connection_row()
{
    delete [] data;
}

//
//          Member function: num_values
//
//          Returns the number of values in this
//          one-dimensional connection_row instance.
//

int connection_row::num_values()
{
    return number_of_values;
}

//
//          operator[]
//
//          Allows references to connection_row elements
//

double & connection_row::operator[](int index)
{
    if (index < 0 || index >= number_of_values)
    {
        cerr << "illegal index: connection_row::operator[]\n";
        exit(1);
    }
    return (double &) data[index];
};
```

The following listing contains the implementation for the connection_weights class.

```
// File: weights.cp
//
// Description: This file contains the C++ implementation of the
//              connection_weights class.
//
//
// This software may be used without restriction in compiled form.
// This source code may not be redistributed without permission.
//
#include <iostream.h>
#include <stdlib.h>
#include "weights.h"

//
//          Class constructor: connection_weights
//

connection_weights::connection_weights(int num_in, int num_out)
```

```
{
    rows = new connection_row * [num_in];
    for (int i=0; i<num_in; i++)
        rows[i] = new connection_row(num_out);
    num_from = num_in;
    num_to   = num_out;
}

//
//          operator[]
//
//          Returns a reference to the connection_row
//          object at index 'input_neuron_index'.
//

connection_row & connection_weights::operator[](int input_neuron_index)
{
    if (input_neuron_index < 0 || input_neuron_index >= num_from)
    {
        cerr << "connection_row & operator[" << input_neuron_index
            << "]: illegal index value\n";
        exit(1);
    }
    return *rows[input_neuron_index];
}
```

The following listing contains the implementation for the `neural_data` class.

```
// File: ndata.cp
//
// Description: This file contains the C++ implementation for
//              the neural_data class.
//
//
// This software may be used without restriction in compiled form.
// This source code may not be redistributed without permission.
//
#include <iostream.h>
#include <fstream.h>
#include <math.h>
#include "ndata.h"
#include "randseq.h"
#include <stdlib.h>

//
//          Function: sigmoid
//
//          See Figure 8.2
//

double sigmoid(double x)
{
    return (1.0 / (1.0 + exp(-x))) - 0.5;
}

//
//          Function: sigmoidP
//
//          See Figure 8.3
//
double sigmoidP(double x)
{
```

```
        double temp = sigmoid(x) + 0.5;
        return temp * (1.0 - temp);
}


//
//            Class constructor #1: neural_data      (3 layers)
//
//
//            Instances of this class contain neuron layers
//            and the connection-strength weight matrices
//            that interconnect neurons in adjacent layers.
//

neural_data::neural_data(int input_size, int hidden_size,
                         int output_size)
{   int i, j;
    inputs = new neuron_layer(input_size);
    hidden_1 = new neuron_layer(hidden_size);
    hidden_2 = (neuron_layer *)NULL;
    outputs = new neuron_layer(output_size);
    num_layers = 3;
    input_layer_size = input_size;
    hidden_1_layer_size = hidden_size;
    hidden_2_layer_size = 0;
    output_layer_size = output_size;
    weights_1 = new connection_weights(input_size, hidden_size);
    weights_2 = new connection_weights(hidden_size, output_size);
    weights_3 = (connection_weights *)NULL;
    RandomSequence random;

    for (i=0; i<input_layer_size; i++)
        for (j=0; j<hidden_1_layer_size; j++)
            (*weights_1)[i][j] = random.rndFP(-0.9, 0.9);
    for (i=0; i<hidden_1_layer_size; i++)
        for (j=0; j<output_layer_size; j++)
            (*weights_2)[i][j] = random.rndFP(-0.9, 0.9);

}


//
//            Class constructor #2: neural_data         (4 layers)
//
//
//            Instances of this class contain neuron layers
//            and the connection-strength weight matrices
//            that interconnect neurons in adjacent layers.
//
neural_data::neural_data(int input_size, int hidden_1_size,
                         int hidden_2_size, int output_size)
{   int i, j;
    inputs = new neuron_layer(input_size);
    hidden_1 = new neuron_layer(hidden_1_size);
    hidden_2 = new neuron_layer(hidden_2_size);
    outputs = new neuron_layer(output_size);
    num_layers = 4;
    input_layer_size = input_size;
    hidden_1_layer_size = hidden_1_size;
    hidden_2_layer_size = hidden_2_size;
    output_layer_size = output_size;
    weights_1 = new connection_weights(input_size, hidden_1_size);
    weights_2 = new connection_weights(hidden_1_size, hidden_2_size);
    weights_3 = new connection_weights(hidden_2_size, output_size);
    RandomSequence random(3.14159);
```

```
        for (i=0; i<input_layer_size; i++)
            for (j=0; j<hidden_1_layer_size; j++)
                (*weights_1)[i][j] = random.rndFP(-0.9, 0.9);
        for (i=0; i<hidden_1_layer_size; i++)
            for (j=0; j<hidden_2_layer_size; j++)
                (*weights_2)[i][j] = random.rndFP(-0.9, 0.9);
        for (i=0; i<hidden_2_layer_size; i++)
            for (j=0; j<output_layer_size; j++)
                (*weights_2)[i][j] = random.rndFP(-0.9, 0.9);
}

neural_data::neural_data(const char * file_name)
{
    inputs = hidden_1 = hidden_2 = outputs = 0;
    int status = restore_from_disk(file_name);
    if (status == -1) {
        cerr << "neural_data::neural_data(" << file_name
             << ") constructor failed.\n";
        exit(1);
    }
}


//
//            Member function: propagate_activations
//
//            Member function propagate_activations is used
//            for implementing the behavior of classes
//            recall_manager and neural_trainer.  The
//            propagation behavior simply takes the activation
//            values of the input layer neurons, uses the first
//            set of connection weights to propagate activations
//            to the first hidden layer, etc.
//

void neural_data::propagate_activations()
{
    int from, to;

    // input layer to first hidden layer:
    for (to=0; to<hidden_1_layer_size; to++)
        (*hidden_1)[to] = 0.0;
    for (from=0; from<input_layer_size; from++)
        for (to=0; to<hidden_1_layer_size; to++)
            (*hidden_1)[to] +=
                (*inputs)[from] * (*weights_1)[from][to];

    if (num_layers == 3)
    {

        // first hidden layer to output layer:
        for (to=0; to<output_layer_size; to++)
            (*outputs)[to] = 0.0;
            for (from=0; from<hidden_1_layer_size; from++)
                for (to=0; to<output_layer_size; to++)
                    (*outputs)[to] +=
                        (*hidden_1)[from] * (*weights_2)[from][to];

    } else
    {   // 4 layer network:

        // first hidden layer to second hidden layer:
        for (to=0; to<hidden_2_layer_size; to++)
            (*hidden_2)[to] = 0.0;
```

```
                    for (from=0; from<hidden_1_layer_size; from++)
                        for (to=0; to<hidden_2_layer_size; to++)
                            (*hidden_2)[to] +=
                                (*hidden_1)[from] * (*weights_2)[from][to];

            // second hidden layer to output layer:
            for (to=0; to<output_layer_size; to++)
                (*outputs)[to] = 0.0;
                for (from=0; from<hidden_2_layer_size; from++)
                    for (to=0; to<output_layer_size; to++)
                        (*outputs)[to] +=
                            (*hidden_2)[from] * (*weights_3)[from][to];

        }

    }


//
//              Member function: save_to_disk
//

int neural_data::save_to_disk(const char * file_name)
{
    int i, j;
    filebuf input_file;

    if (input_file.open(file_name, ios::out) == 0)
    {
        cerr << "neural_data::save_to_disk: could not open file "
            << file_name << "\n";
        return -1;
    }
    ostream out_stream(&input_file);
    out_stream << num_layers << " ";
    out_stream << input_layer_size << " ";
    out_stream << hidden_1_layer_size << " ";
    out_stream << hidden_2_layer_size << " ";
    out_stream << output_layer_size << "\n";

    if (num_layers == 3)
    {
        for (i=0; i<input_layer_size; i++)
        {
            out_stream << "\n";
            for (j=0; j<hidden_1_layer_size; j++)
                out_stream << (*weights_1)[i][j] << " ";
        }
        for (i=0; i<hidden_1_layer_size; i++)
        {
            out_stream << "\n";
            for (j=0; j<output_layer_size; j++)
                out_stream << (*weights_2)[i][j] << " ";
        }
    } else
    { // four layers:
        for (i=0; i<input_layer_size; i++)
            for (j=0; j<hidden_1_layer_size; j++)
                out_stream << (*weights_1)[i][j] << " ";
        for (i=0; i<hidden_1_layer_size; i++)
            for (j=0; j<hidden_2_layer_size; j++)
                out_stream << (*weights_2)[i][j] << " ";
        for (i=0; i<hidden_2_layer_size; i++)
            for (j=0; j<output_layer_size; j++)
                out_stream << (*weights_3)[i][j] << " ";
```

```
        }
        return 0;
}

//
//              Member function: restore_from_disk
//
int neural_data::restore_from_disk(const char * file_name)
{
    delete inputs;
    delete hidden_1;
    delete hidden_2;
    delete outputs;

    int i, j;
    filebuf input_file;

    if (input_file.open(file_name, ios::in) == 0)
    {
        cerr << "neural_data::restore_from_disk: could not open file "
             << file_name << "\n";
        return -1;
    }
    istream in_stream(&input_file);
    in_stream >> num_layers;
    in_stream >> input_layer_size;
    in_stream >> hidden_1_layer_size;
    in_stream >> hidden_2_layer_size;
    in_stream >> output_layer_size;

    inputs = new neuron_layer(input_layer_size);
    hidden_1 = new neuron_layer(hidden_1_layer_size);
    outputs = new neuron_layer(output_layer_size);


    if (num_layers == 3)
    {
        weights_1 =
          new connection_weights(input_layer_size, hidden_1_layer_size);
        weights_2 =
          new connection_weights(hidden_1_layer_size, output_layer_size);
        weights_3 = (connection_weights *)NULL;
        for (i=0; i<input_layer_size; i++)
            for (j=0; j<hidden_1_layer_size; j++)
                in_stream >> (*weights_1)[i][j];
        for (i=0; i<hidden_1_layer_size; i++)
            for (j=0; j<output_layer_size; j++)
                in_stream >> (*weights_2)[i][j];
    } else  // four layers:
    {   // four layers:
        hidden_2 = new neuron_layer(hidden_2_layer_size);
        weights_1 =
          new connection_weights(input_layer_size, hidden_1_layer_size);
        weights_2 =
          new connection_weights(hidden_1_layer_size, hidden_2_layer_size);
        weights_3 =
          new connection_weights(hidden_2_layer_size, output_layer_size);
        for (i=0; i<input_layer_size; i++)
            for (j=0; j<hidden_1_layer_size; j++)
                in_stream >> (*weights_1)[i][j];
        for (i=0; i<hidden_1_layer_size; i++)
            for (j=0; j<hidden_2_layer_size; j++)
                in_stream >> (*weights_2)[i][j];
        for (i=0; i<hidden_2_layer_size; i++)
```

```
                for (j=0; j<output_layer_size; j++)
                    in_stream >> (*weights_3)[i][j];
        }

    return 0;
}


//
//          Member function: set_inputs
//
//          Sets the input neuron activation values from
//          the values in the connection input_values.
//

void neural_data::set_inputs(connection_row &input_values)
{
    if (input_layer_size != input_values.num_values())
    {
        cerr << "neural_data::set_inputs: size mismatch\n";
        cerr << "input_layer_size=" << input_layer_size << "\n";
        cerr << "input_values.num_values()="
             << input_values.num_values() << "\n";
        exit(1);
    }
    for (int i=0; i<input_layer_size; i++)
        (*inputs)[i] = input_values[i];
}


//
//          Member function: set_inputs
//
//          Sets the input neuron activation values from
//          the values in the neuron_layer input_values.
//

void neural_data::set_inputs(neuron_layer &input_values)
{
    if (input_layer_size != input_values.num_neurons())
    {
        cerr << "neural_data::set_inputs: size mismatch\n";
        cerr << "input_layer_size=" << input_layer_size << "\n";
        cerr << "input_values.num_neurons()="
             << input_values.num_neurons() << "\n";
        exit(1);
    }
    for (int i=0; i<input_layer_size; i++)
        (*inputs)[i] = input_values[i];
}


//
//          Member function: read_outputs
//
//          Copies the current activation energy values in
//          the output layer neurons to the neuron_layer
//          output_values.
//

void neural_data::read_outputs(neuron_layer &output_values)
{
    if (output_layer_size != output_values.num_neurons())
    {
        cerr << "neural_data::read_outputs: size mismatch\n";
        exit(1);
    }
```

```
        for (int i=0; i<output_layer_size; i++)
            output_values[i] = (*outputs)[i];
    }
```

The functions `sigmoid` and `sigmoidP` are described in Sec. 8.1 and are plotted in Figure 8.2. The class `neural_data` has three constructors, as described in Sec. 9.2.

The member function `propagate_activations` is a utility function for propagating activation values through a neural network. Figure 9.2 shows how this is done for a very simple network.

The member functions `save_to_disk` and `restore_from_disk` are simple. They simply write or read the network size and values of the connection weights to ".net" network files. Notice that we do not bother to save neuron activation values, since the knowledge stored in neural networks is stored in the connection-weight strengths.

The member function `set_inputs` is overloaded for two types of arguments: `connection_row &` and `neuron_layer &`.

The following listing contains the implementation for the `neural_trainer` class.

```
// File: trainer.cp
//
// Description: This file contains the C++ implementation for the
//              class neural_trainer. An instance of this class
//              is used to create a trained neural_data object,
//              which can be saved to disk as a persistent object
//              for later use. Note: the constructor for this class
//              does it all—reads the training data, trains the
//              network, saves the network to disk, and frees memory.
//
//
// This software may be used without restriction in compiled form.
// This source code may not be redistributed without permission.
//
#include <iostream.h>
#include <fstream.h>
#include <stdlib.h>
```

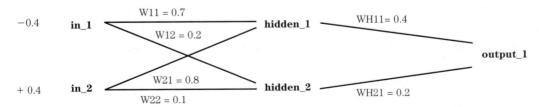

Input neuron layer: **Hidden neuron layer:**   **Output neuron layer:**

Figure 9.2 A three-layer neural network with two input neurons, two hidden neurons, and one output neuron. The new activation energy of a neuron is equal to the sigmoid of the sum of the products of input activation energies and the connection-strength weights. For example, with input values of –0.4 for input neuron in_1 and +0.4 for input neuron in_2, the new activation energy of hidden neuron hidden_1 is `sigmoid( in_1 * W11 + in_2 * W21)`. In this case, the activation energy of the hidden_1 neuron is equal to `sigmoid( -0.4 * 0.7 + 0.4 * 0.8)`.

```cpp
#include "ndata.h"
#include "trainer.h"
#include "randseq.h"

double sigmoid(double x);    // see Figure 8.2
double sigmoidP(double x);   // see Figure 8.3

//
//          Class constructor: neural_trainer
//

neural_trainer::neural_trainer(const char *input_training_data_set_name,
                               const char *output_trained_neural_data_name)
{
    int num_layers, input_layer_size, hidden_1_layer_size;
    int hidden_2_layer_size, output_layer_size, num_examples;
    int i, j, k, from, to;

    RandomSequence random;

    filebuf input_file;
    if (input_file.open(input_training_data_set_name, ios::in) == 0)
    {
        cerr << "neural_data::neural_trainer: could not open file "
            << input_training_data_set_name << "\n";
        exit(1);
    }
    istream in_stream(&input_file);
    // skip any comment lines beginning with a # character:
    char buf[81];
    if (in_stream.peek() == '#') in_stream.getline(buf, 80, '\n');
    if (in_stream.peek() == '#') in_stream.getline(buf, 80, '\n');
    if (in_stream.peek() == '#') in_stream.getline(buf, 80, '\n');
    if (in_stream.peek() == '#') in_stream.getline(buf, 80, '\n');
    in_stream >> num_layers;
    in_stream.ignore(80, '\n');
    if (in_stream.peek() == '#') in_stream.getline(buf, 80, '\n');
    if (in_stream.peek() == '#') in_stream.getline(buf, 80, '\n');
    if (in_stream.peek() == '#') in_stream.getline(buf, 80, '\n');
    if (in_stream.peek() == '#') in_stream.getline(buf, 80, '\n');
    in_stream >> input_layer_size;
    in_stream.ignore(80, '\n');
    if (in_stream.peek() == '#') in_stream.getline(buf, 80, '\n');
    if (in_stream.peek() == '#') in_stream.getline(buf, 80, '\n');
    if (in_stream.peek() == '#') in_stream.getline(buf, 80, '\n');
    in_stream >> hidden_1_layer_size;
    in_stream.ignore(80, '\n');
    if (in_stream.peek() == '#') in_stream.getline(buf, 80, '\n');
    if (in_stream.peek() == '#') in_stream.getline(buf, 80, '\n');
    in_stream >> hidden_2_layer_size;
    in_stream.ignore(80, '\n');
    if (in_stream.peek() == '#') in_stream.getline(buf, 80, '\n');
    if (in_stream.peek() == '#') in_stream.getline(buf, 80, '\n');
    in_stream >> output_layer_size;
    in_stream.ignore(80, '\n');
    if (in_stream.peek() == '#') in_stream.getline(buf, 80, '\n');
    if (in_stream.peek() == '#') in_stream.getline(buf, 80, '\n');

    in_stream >> num_examples;
    in_stream.ignore(80, '\n');
    if (in_stream.peek() == '#') in_stream.getline(buf, 80, '\n');
    if (in_stream.peek() == '#') in_stream.getline(buf, 80, '\n');
    if (in_stream.peek() == '#') in_stream.getline(buf, 80, '\n');
    if (in_stream.peek() == '#') in_stream.getline(buf, 80, '\n');
```

```
#ifdef DEBUG
    cerr << "num_layers = " << num_layers << ", input size ="
         << input_layer_size << ", hidden_1_layer_size ="
         << hidden_1_layer_size << ", output size ="
         << output_layer_size << "\n";
#endif

    neuron_layer inputs(input_layer_size);
    neuron_layer hidden_1(hidden_1_layer_size);
    neuron_layer outputs(output_layer_size);

    neuron_layer hidden_1_errors(hidden_1_layer_size);
    neuron_layer output_errors(output_layer_size);

    // use connection_weight 2D array: for holding the training examples
    connection_weights example_inputs(num_examples, input_layer_size);
    connection_weights example_outputs(num_examples, output_layer_size);


    for (k=0; k<num_examples; k++)
    {
        // read in alternating row of inputs and outputs:
        for (i=0; i<input_layer_size; i++)
            in_stream >> example_inputs[k][i];
        for (j=0; j<output_layer_size; j++)
            in_stream >> example_outputs[k][j];
    }

#ifdef DEBUG
    cerr << "\ndone reading samples from file.  Example:\n\n";
    for (k=0; k<num_examples; k++)
    {
        for (i=0; i<input_layer_size; i++)
            cerr <<   example_inputs[k][i] << "   ";
        cerr << "  outputs: ";
        for (i=0; i<output_layer_size; i++)
            cerr << example_outputs[k][i] << "   ";
        cerr << "\n";
    }
#endif

    // Check for the (simpler) three-layer case:
    if (hidden_2_layer_size == -1 ||
        hidden_2_layer_size == 0)

    { // 3 layer case

        int max_iters = 15 + num_examples*input_layer_size*output_layer_size;
        double rms_error;

        // create a neural_data object to train:
        neural_data nn(input_layer_size,
                       hidden_1_layer_size, output_layer_size);

        for (int iter=0; iter<max_iters; iter++)
        {

#ifdef DEBUG
            cerr << "* * starting learning iteration " << iter;
#endif

            rms_error = 0.0;

            for (int example=0; example<num_examples; example++)
```

```
            {
                // zero out entire layer:
                hidden_1_errors.set_layer_values(0.0);
                // zero out entire layer:
                output_errors.set_layer_values(0.0);
                nn.set_inputs(example_inputs[example]);
                nn.propagate_activations();
                // accumulate error in the output layer:
                for (j=0; j<output_layer_size; j++)
                    output_errors[j] +=
            (example_outputs[example][j] -
                                    sigmoid((*nn.outputs)[j]))
                                * sigmoidP((*nn.outputs)[j]);
                // accumulate hidden_1 errors:
                for (i=0; i<hidden_1_layer_size; i++)
                {
                    hidden_1_errors[i] = 0.0;
                    for (j=0; j<output_layer_size; j++)
                        hidden_1_errors[i] +=
                                        output_errors[j]
                                    * (*nn.weights_2)[i][j];
                }
                for (i=0; i<hidden_1_layer_size; i++)
                    hidden_1_errors[i] = hidden_1_errors[i]
                                * sigmoidP((*nn.hidden_1)[i]);
                // update the hidden_1 to output layer weights:
                for (j=0; j<output_layer_size; j++)
                    for (i=0; i<hidden_1_layer_size; i++)
                        (*nn.weights_2)[i][j] +=
                            0.7 * output_errors[j] * (*nn.hidden_1)[i];
                // update the input layer to hidden layer weights:
                for (j=0; j<hidden_1_layer_size; j++)
                    for (i=0; i<input_layer_size; i++)
                        (*nn.weights_1)[i][j] +=
                            0.7 * hidden_1_errors[j] * (*nn.inputs)[i];
                for (j=0; j<output_layer_size; j++)
                    rms_error += output_errors[j] * output_errors[j];
            }
#ifdef DEBUG
            cerr << "  rms_error = " << rms_error << "\n";
#endif
        }
        nn.save_to_disk(output_trained_neural_data_name);
    }
        else
    {   // four-layer case (2 hidden layers):
        neuron_layer hidden_2_errors(hidden_2_layer_size);
        connection_weights weights_2(hidden_1_layer_size, hidden_2_layer_size);
        connection_weights weights_3(hidden_2_layer_size, output_layer_size);

        int max_iters = 15 + num_examples*input_layer_size*output_layer_size;
        double rms_error;

        // create a neural_data object to train:
        neural_data nn(input_layer_size,
                    hidden_1_layer_size, hidden_2_layer_size,
                    output_layer_size);

        for (int iter=0; iter<max_iters; iter++)
        {

#ifdef DEBUG
            cerr << "* * starting learning iteration " << iter;
#endif
```

```
            rms_error = 0.0;

            for (int example=0; example<num_examples; example++)
            {
                // zero out entire layer for both hidden neuron layers:
                hidden_1_errors.set_layer_values(0.0);
                hidden_2_errors.set_layer_values(0.0);
                // zero out entire output layer:
                output_errors.set_layer_values(0.0);
                nn.set_inputs(example_inputs[example]);
                nn.propagate_activations();
                // accumulate error in the output layer:
                for (j=0; j<output_layer_size; j++)
                    output_errors[j] +=              (example_outputs[example][j] -
                                        sigmoid((*nn.outputs)[j]))
                                    * sigmoidP((*nn.outputs)[j]);
                // accumulate hidden_2 errors:
                for (i=0; i<hidden_2_layer_size; i++)
                {
                    hidden_2_errors[i] = 0.0;
                    for (j=0; j<output_layer_size; j++)
                        hidden_2_errors[i] +=
                                            output_errors[j]
                                        * (*nn.weights_3)[i][j];
                }
                // accumulate hidden_1 errors:
                for (i=0; i<hidden_1_layer_size; i++)
                {
                    hidden_1_errors[i] = 0.0;
                    for (j=0; j<output_layer_size; j++)
                        hidden_1_errors[i] +=
                                            hidden_2_errors[j]
                                        * (*nn.weights_2)[i][j];
                }
                for (i=0; i<hidden_2_layer_size; i++)
                    hidden_2_errors[i] = hidden_2_errors[i]
                                    * sigmoidP((*nn.hidden_2)[i]);
                for (i=0; i<hidden_1_layer_size; i++)
                    hidden_1_errors[i] = hidden_1_errors[i]
                                    * sigmoidP((*nn.hidden_1)[i]);
                // update the hidden_2 to output layer weights:
                for (j=0; j<output_layer_size; j++)
                    for (i=0; i<hidden_2_layer_size; i++)
                        (*nn.weights_3)[i][j] +=
                            0.7 * output_errors[j] * (*nn.hidden_2)[i];
                // update the hidden_1 to hidden_2 layer weights:
                for (j=0; j<hidden_2_layer_size; j++)
                    for (i=0; i<hidden_1_layer_size; i++)
                        (*nn.weights_2)[i][j] +=
                            0.7 * hidden_2_errors[j] * (*nn.hidden_1)[i];
                // update the input layer to hidden_1 layer weights:
                for (j=0; j<hidden_1_layer_size; j++)
                    for (i=0; i<input_layer_size; i++)
                        (*nn.weights_1)[i][j] +=
                            0.7 * hidden_1_errors[j] * (*nn.inputs)[i];
                for (j=0; j<output_layer_size; j++)
                    rms_error += output_errors[j] * output_errors[j];
            }
#ifdef DEBUG
            cerr << "  rms_error = " << rms_error << "\n";
#endif
        }
        nn.save_to_disk(output_trained_neural_data_name);      }
}
```

```
//
//          Class constructor: neural_trainer
//
neural_trainer::~neural_trainer()
{
}
```

As we saw in Sec. 9.2, the constructor for class `neural_trainer` has two required `const char *` arguments: the name of a training file and the name of a ".net" network file to use for saving the trained neural network. This class constructor has the interesting and important behavior of training a `neural_data` object (i.e., finding values for the connection-strength objects) based on the data in a training file. There are two sections of code for training, one for three-layer networks and one for four-layer networks. The following steps are required for training a three-layer network:

- For each training example:
- zero out the error arrays for the hidden and output neuron layers
- set the input values from the training example
- propagate the new input neuron activation values through the network to the output neuron layer
- for each output neuron, calculate the error for that neuron as:

```
(example value - propagated value) * sigmoidP(sum of hidden values * weights)
```

- for each hidden neuron h, calculate the error as:

```
sum over output neurons o of:
hidden_error[h] += output_errors[o] * hidden_to_output_weights[j][o]
```

- scale the hidden error for each hidden neuron by multiplying it by the activation energy value of the hidden neuron
- update the hidden to output weights by adding the output errors times the hidden activations
- update the input to hidden weights by adding the hidden neuron layer errors times the input neuron activation energy

This sequence of steps is repeated many times (reusing the same training examples) until the network is trained to match the desired training output values for each training input example.

Application note: When to use a four-layer network

This class library supports both three- and four-layer neural networks. Three-layer networks are capable of learning complex patterns, but they cannot always learn arbitrary mappings between desired training input and output patterns. Four-layer networks can learn arbitrary mappings if they have a sufficient number of hidden neurons in both of their hidden neuron layers.

Still, you should avoid using four-layer networks. In general, four-layer networks take many more training iterations than do three-layer networks. Also, when embedded in your applications, four-layer neural networks run slightly slower and require more storage space.

My advice is to start by building your training set (see Chapters 10 and 11 for many examples). Then always try to train a three-layer network first. You can tell whether a network is learning all of its training example patterns by turning on DEBUG printout and watching the value of RMS_error that is printed for each training cycle. This error should get very close to zero. If the error does not eventually get very small, then try specifying a four-layer network in your training file.

The following listing contains the implementation for the recall_manager class.

```cpp
// File: recall.cp
//
// Description: This file contains the C++ implementation for
//              the recall_manager class.
//
//
// This software may be used without restriction in compiled form.
// This source code may not be redistributed without permission.
//
#include <iostream.h>
#include "recall.h"
#include "nlayer.h"

double sigmoid(double);  // see Figure 8.2

//
//          Class constructor: recall_manager
//

recall_manager::recall_manager(const char * neural_data_file)
{
    data = new neural_data(neural_data_file);
    outputs = new neuron_layer(data->outputs->num_neurons());
}

//
//          Class destructor: recall_manager
//
recall_manager::~recall_manager()
{
    delete data;
    delete outputs;
}

//
//          Member function: calculate_outputs
//
//          Given a new set of input layer neuron values,
//          copy them to the input neurons, and propagate
```

```
//            activation values through connection weights
//            and hidden layer neurons to the output layer
//            neurons.
//

void recall_manager::calculate_outputs(neuron_layer &new_inputs)
{
    data->set_inputs(new_inputs);   // does size error checking
    data->propagate_activations();
}


//
//            operator[]
//
//            Note: this is an unusual (but useful) use of
//                  operator[].  Here, it simply returns
//                  the current activation energy of the
//                  neuron in the output layer with the
//                  index output_neuron_index.
//

double recall_manager::operator[](int output_neuron_index)
{
    return sigmoid((*data->outputs)[output_neuron_index]);
}
```

Compared to with the `neural_trainer` class, the `recall_manager` class is very simple. You will use instances of the `recall_manager` class when you embed neural networks in your applications.

The constructor for the `recall_manager` class has one required argument: the name of a ".net" network save file. A `recall_manager` object simply uses the constructor for a `neural_data` object to create a `neural_data` object from the specified ".net" file. The member function `calculate_outputs` takes a set of new activation energies and copies them to the input `neuron_layer` neurons. Then the `neural_data` member function `propagate_activations` is used to propagate the specified input pattern to the output `neuron_layer` neurons.

The operator `operator[](int output_neuron_index)` provides convenient access to the output pattern (or output activation energy values) after using member function `calculate_outputs`.

Applicaton Example:
Neural Network Classifier
for Making Buy/No-Buy Decisions
for Home Consumer Goods

In Chapter 8, I discussed the concept of defining a neural network architecture by creating an input neuron for each input parameter and an output neuron for each desired system output. A neural network is trained by providing a set of input and desired output training examples that are used to alter the internal state of the network, producing a mapping between system inputs and outputs. As we saw in Chapter 8, if the set of training examples is large enough, the network learns to generalize by learning to ignore noise in the input data, "concentrating" instead on key features of the input data that were most useful in distinguishing the original training data sets.

10.1 Desired Neural Network Input and Output Values

You learned in Chapter 8 that the neurons in our network have output activation values in the range –0.5 to 0.5. It is important that you map your input values to this same range.

I want to classify consumer goods based on a set of parameters. I suggest the following set of input parameters to start with, but you should feel free to add more of your own:

- cost
- practical use
- entertainment value

- tax deductible
- multiple-person use
- impulse buy flag

It is often challenging to map a set of arbitrary input values to a numerical range from –0.5 to 0.5. Fortunately, neural networks deal very well with nonlinear relationships among network inputs. This allows us to use a nonlinear mapping of input values to the range –0.5 to 0.5. Also, it is usually preferable not to specify network training input and output values at the extreme values –0.5 and 0.5; rather scale them instead to the range –0.4 to 0.4. I will use the mapping shown in Table 10.1 for the cost of consumer items.

TABLE 10.1 Mapping Purchase Costs into Neural Network Input Neuron Values

Cost (in $)	Neural network training value
0–5	–0.4
6–25	–0.3
26–100	–0.2
101–500	–0.1
501–2000	0.0
2000–10000	0.2
10001–9999999	0.4

In the application, I use linear interpolation within these input ranges. For example, between $5 and $25, I calculate the "cost" input neurons value as:

```
cost(dollar_value) = -0.4 + (dollar_value - 5.0) * ( 0.1) / (25 - 5)
```

The estimate of "practical use" is subjective, and is entered in the range –0.4 to 0.4.

The estimate of "entertainment value" is also subjective, and is entered in the range –0.4 to 0.4.

The "tax deductible" flag is binary, and is entered either as the value –0.4 if the item is not tax deductible, or as 0.4 if the item is tax deductible.

The "multiple-person use" flag is also binary and is entered either as the value –0.4 if only one person will use this item, or as 0.4 if more than one person will use this item.

The "impulse buy" flag is binary, and is set to –0.4 if you seriously planned to buy this item for more than one day before the purchase, or is set to 0.4 if this item was purchased on impulse.

Inputs: Output:

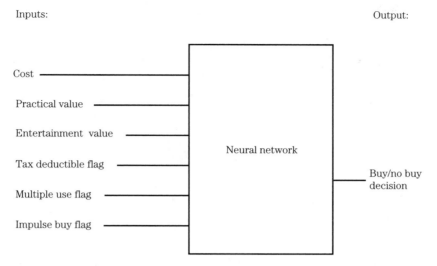

Figure 10.1   External architecture of a neural network to evaluate consumer purchases.

10.2   System Output

The neural network to solve this application problem will have a single output value. When you set up training examples, after you have used your purchased item, decide whether you wish you had not bought the item (then the training output is set to –0.4), or are you pleased with your purchase (in which case you set the training output to 0.4). Figure 10.1 shows the network architecture.

10.3   Training Data

The following listing shows the file train.dat located in the ch10 directory on the software disk. Notice that optional comment lines start with a # sign.

```
# number of layers in the neural network:
3
# number of neurons in the input layer:
6
# number of neurons in the first hidden layer:
4
# number of neurons in the second hidden layer:
0
# number of neurons in the output layer:
1
# number of training examples:
20
#  cost   practical   entertain   tax deduct   multiple use   impulse buy   Good?
#  ----   ---------   ---------   ----------   ------------   -----------   -----

   0.0      -0.1         0.2         0.4           0.4           -0.4        0.2
   0.0      -0.1         0.2         0.4           0.4            0.4       -0.2
```

0.0	-0.1	0.4	0.4	0.4	0.4	0.1
0.0	-0.3	0.2	0.4	0.4	-0.4	-0.1
0.0	-0.3	0.2	0.4	0.4	0.4	-0.3
-0.3	-0.3	0.2	0.4	0.4	-0.4	0.3
0.0	0.4	0.2	0.4	0.4	-0.4	0.4
0.0	0.4	0.2	0.4	0.4	-0.4	0.4
0.3	0.4	0.2	0.4	0.4	-0.4	0.1
0.0	0.4	0.2	0.4	0.4	-0.4	0.4
0.0	0.4	0.2	-0.4	0.4	-0.4	0.2
0.0	0.1	-0.1	0.4	0.4	-0.4	0.3
0.0	0.1	-0.1	0.4	0.4	-0.4	0.3
0.0	0.1	-0.1	0.4	0.4	-0.4	0.3
-0.1	-0.2	-0.1	-0.4	-0.4	0.4	-0.2
-0.1	-0.2	0.3	-0.4	-0.4	0.4	0.1
-0.1	-0.2	-0.1	-0.4	-0.4	-0.4	0.2
-0.3	-0.2	-0.1	-0.4	-0.4	0.4	0.0
0.3	-0.2	-0.1	-0.4	-0.4	0.4	-0.4
-0.2	-0.3	0.2	-0.4	-0.4	0.4	-0.2

10.4 Example Program

The sample program is very simple. The real work is done in the neural network class libraries developed in Chapter 9.

```
// File: ch10.cp
//
// Description: This file contains the example program for
//              Chapter 10. The file train.dat in the ch10
//              directory on the software disk is used for
//              training.
//
//

#include "recall.h"
#include "trainer.h"

#include <iostream.h>
#include <fstream.h>
#include <stdlib.h>
#include <string.h>


void main()
{
    cerr << "Initial simple test for Chapter 10 example:\n\n";

    // Create a neural trainer object using the text file "train.dat"
    // for specifying the network size and training data:

    neural_trainer nt("train.dat", "train.net");

    // Create a recall_manager object to use the trained neural
    // network which the neural_trainer object saved to file
    // "train.net":

    recall_manager rm("train.net");

    // Test the network:
```

```
        cerr << "Test network trained by data in 'train.dat':\n\n";

        neuron_layer nl(6);

        cerr << "Possible purchase: Color TV:\n\n";
        cerr << "  Cost = $450\n";
        cerr << "  Entertainment value = High\n";
        cerr << "  Tax deductible = NO\n";
        cerr << "  Multiple use = YES (by everyone in the family)\n";
        cerr << "  Impulse buy  = NO\n\n";

        nl[0] = 0.1;  nl[1] = 0.4;  nl[2] = -0.4;
        nl[3] = 0.4;  nl[4] = 0.3;  nl[5] = -0.3;

        rm.calculate_outputs(nl);

        cerr << "Output from trained neural network (range: -0.5 - 0.5): "
             << rm[0] << "\n\n";

        if (rm[0] < -0.1)
            cerr << "Recommend against purchase\n";
        else if (rm[0] < 0.1)
            cerr << "No decision possible\n";
        else
            cerr << "Purchase recommended\n";

    }
```

The following listing shows the various outputs of this test program (compiled without the DEBUG flag set).

```
Initial simple test for chapter 10 example:

Test network trained by data in 'train.dat':

Possible purchase: Color TV:

  Cost = $450
  Entertainment value = High
  Tax deductible = NO
  Multiple use = YES (by everyone in the family)
  Impulse buy  = NO

Output from trained neural network (range: -0.5 - 0.5): 0.272799

Purchase recommended
```

The following is from a similar execution, with the impulse buy flag set to YES.

```
Initial simple test for Chapter 10 example:

Test network trained by data in 'train.dat':

Possible purchase: Color TV:

  Cost = $450
  Entertainment value = High
  Tax deductible = NO
  Multiple use = YES (by everyone in the family)
```

```
Impulse buy  = YES

Output from trained neural network (range: -0.5 - 0.5): 0.087202

No decision possible
```

The following run was modified for a single adult purchaser (no multiple use).

```
Initial simple test for Chapter 10 example:

Test network trained by data in 'train.dat':

Possible purchase: Color TV:

  Cost = $450
  Entertainment value = High
  Tax deductible = NO
  Multiple use = NO
  Impulse buy  = YES

Output from trained neural network (range: -0.5 - 0.5): -0.152493

Recommend against purchase
```

These examples are simple, but they demonstrate:

- setting up a neural network training data file for a `neural_trainer` object
- mapping application-specific values into inputs acceptable by a neural network
- interpreting numeric values of output neuron(s) correctly for an application

As you have seen in this chapter, it is easy to use the C++ neural network classes to train a network and to embed it in an application. The difficult part of this process is preparing the training data.

11

Application Example: Neural Network Controller for a Hypothetical Factory

Neural networks have been successfully used for controlling factory equipment, robotics arms, etc. The back propagation neural network C++ class library developed in Chapter 9 is not appropriate for systems that require analog outputs. The hypothetical factory equipment that I simulate in this chapter only requires on–off controls. The example program developed in this chapter has two logical modules: a factory simulation module, and a neural network control module. To make the operation of the factory simulator simple, it will use data files to determine its state. Most of the work involved in creating the simulation will be creating these data files for initial training, and a separate set for testing.

11.1 The Simulated Factory

We simulate a factory with the equipment shown in Figure 11.1.

11.2 Simulation of a Simple Factory

There are three ways to test the concept of using a neural network in this test problem:

1. Simulate the desired behavior of sensors and control by reading values calculated *ad hoc* by hand from a data file.

2. Write a software simulation of a factory that uses randomly generated events in a simulation of a physical model of a real factory. Figure 11.2 shows one possible class structure for writing a simulation.

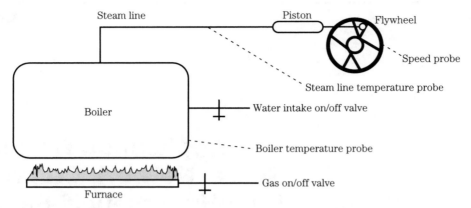

Figure 11.1 Simulated factory equipment with two controls and three probes. The three probes are inputs to the neural network, and the two control valves are the neural network outputs.

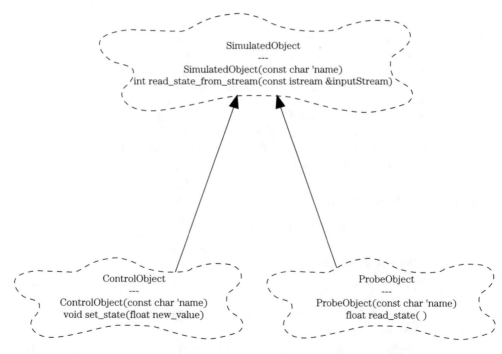

Figure 11.2 Class diagram for the factory simulation. The simulation objects gas on/off valve and water intake on/off valve will be instances of class `ControlObject`. The simulation objects boiler temperature probe, steam line temperature probe, and speed probe will be instances of class `ProbeObject`.

3. Instrument a real factory. Record real sensor readings and the responses from human operators to collect training data for a neural network.

For simplicity, I use the first option: reading values from a training file.

11.3 Using Data Files to Simulate Factory

I use a text data file containing both the values of the control inputs (boiler temperature, steam line temperature, and flywheel speed) and the desired control outputs (gas on/off control, water intake on/off valve). The following listing shows the file train.dat that is located in the directory ch11 on the software disk.

```
# number of layers in the neural network:
3
# number of neurons in the input layer:
3
# number of neurons in the first hidden layer:
3
# number of neurons in the second hidden layer:
0
#number of neurons in the output layer:
2
# number of training examples:
10
#  Boiler temp    steam temp    speed     gas control     water control
#  ----------     ----------    -----     -----------     -------------
           -0.4          -0.4    -0.4            0.4               -0.4
           -0.2          -0.3    -0.4            0.4               -0.4
           -0.1          -0.2    -0.4            0.4               -0.4
           -0.1          -0.1    -0.3            0.4               -0.4

            0.2           0.1     0.3           -0.4               -0.4
            0.3           0.2     0.4           -0.4               -0.4
            0.1           0.2     0.3           -0.4               -0.4

            0.4          -0.2    -0.2           -0.4                0.4
            0.3          -0.3    -0.3           -0.4                0.4
            0.3          -0.4    -0.4           -0.4                0.4
```

This file is readable by a `neural_trainer` object (class developed in Chapter 9). The following listing shows the implementation of the factory controller example (file ch11.cp in directory ch11 on the software disk). Note that almost all of the interesting behavior of this example program is provided by the neural network class library developed in Chapter 9.

```
// File: ch11.cp
//
// Description: This file contains the factory automation neural
//              network example from Chapter 11.
//
//

#include "recall.h"
#include "trainer.h"
```

```
#include <iostream.h>
#include <fstream.h>
#include <stdlib.h>
#include <string.h>


static const char * convert_temperature_to_english(float temperature)
{
    if (temperature < -0.3)  return "very cold temperature";
    if (temperature < -0.1)  return "cold temperature";
    if (temperature <  0.1)  return "slightly warm";
    if (temperature <  0.3)  return "warm (nominal temperature)";
    return "too hot";
}

static const char * convert_speed_to_english(float speed)
{
    if (speed < -0.3)  return "stopped";
    if (speed < -0.1)  return "very slow";
    if (speed <  0.1)  return "slow";
    if (speed <  0.3)  return "nominal temperature";
    return "too fast";
}

static void test_helper(recall_manager &rm,
                        float boiler_temperature,
                        float steam_temperature,
                        float speed)
{
    neuron_layer nl(3);
    nl[0] = boiler_temperature;
    nl[1] = steam_temperature;
    nl[2] = speed;

    cerr << "\ninput boiler temperature: "
         << convert_temperature_to_english(boiler_temperature)
         << "\n";
    cerr << "input steam temperature: "
         << convert_temperature_to_english(steam_temperature)
         << "\n";
    cerr << "input speed reading: "
         << convert_speed_to_english(speed) << "\n";

    rm.calculate_outputs(nl);

    cerr << "Recommended: gas control value   = " << rm[0] << "\n";
    cerr << "             water control value = " << rm[1] << "\n";
}


void main()
{
    // Create a neural trainer object using the text file "train.dat"
    // for specifying the network size and training data:

    neural_trainer("train.dat", "train.net");

    // Create a recall manager object to use the trained neural
    // network which the neural trainer object saved to file
    // "train.net":

    recall_manager rm("train.net");

    // Test the network:
```

```
        test_helper(rm,  -0.3,  -0.2,  -0.3);
        test_helper(rm,   0.2,   0.3,   0.3);
        test_helper(rm,   0.3,  -0.3,  -0.3);
        test_helper(rm,   0.4,   0.2,  -0.3);
}
```

11.4 Example Program Output

The following listing shows the output from the program in Sec. 11.3.

```
input boiler temperature: very cold temperature
input steam temperature: cold temperature
input speed reading: stopped
Recommended: gas control value   =  0.463647
             water control value = -0.140213

input boiler temperature: warm (nominal temperature)
input steam temperature: too hot
input speed reading: too fast
Recommended: gas control value   = -0.428463
             water control value =  0.059575

input boiler temperature: too hot
input steam temperature: very cold temperature
input speed reading: stopped
Recommended: gas control value   = -0.355308
             water control value =  0.288985

input boiler temperature: too hot
input steam temperature: warm (nominal temperature)
input speed reading: stopped
Recommended: gas control value   = -0.468152
             water control value =  0.318239
```

Using Genetic Algorithms to Train Neural Networks

Training Recurrent Neural Networks with Genetic Algorithms

You have now seen that neural networks can be used to solve pattern-recognition and control problems. Problems with continuous input data require neural networks with feedback loops between neuron layers, which are called recurrent neural networks (Rumelhart and McClelland, 1986). Figure 12.1 shows a simple recurrent network.

In this chapter you will see how to search for a set of weights for a recurrent neural network by treating the set of weights as a chromosome, and you will use a genetic algorithm to find a "fit" chromosome that minimizes the error for a given set of neural network training data.

Training neural networks with the example genetic algorithm programs in this chapter takes much longer than the software developed in Chapter 9. The advantage in using genetic algorithms lies in the ability to design arbitrarily connected neural networks, and train them, without requiring a formal scheme for adapting the connection weight values for a set of training data.

I begin this chapter with two simple problems that can be more efficiently solved using the neural network classes developed in Chapter 9. I then apply genetic algorithm based training to an artificial life problem: an ant, with limited sensor ability, learns to find food in an efficient way. This problem can only be solved with a recurrent neural network, or its computational equivalent. In this chapter I train a recurrent network to program an artificial ant to find food efficiently. (Koza (1992) describes a similar experiment conducted by David Jefferson, Robert Collins, Claus Cooper, Michael Dyer, Margot Flowers, Richard Korf, Charles Taylor, and Alan Wang.)

This chapter contains two similar example programs that are both used to solve the same three sample problems. The first example program uses fixed-length

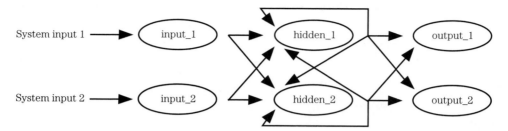

Figure 12.1 A recurrent neural network with two hidden-layer neurons whose outputs feed back to each neuron in the hidden layer (in addition to feeding forward to the output-layer neurons).

weights in the chromosomes. In the second example program, I introduce a new technique, VariGenSearch™, for optimizing the genetic search in the huge search space defined by the set of possible weights for a neural network. This technique varies the chromosome size during training.

Although Rumelhart and McClelland (1986) extend the back-propagation learning rules (which we saw implemented in our neural network classes in Chapter 9) to recurrent neural networks, genetic algorithms provide a good alternative solution to finding values for the connection weights in recurrent neural networks.

12.1 Representing Neural Network Connection Weights in a Genetic Algorithm

In principle, the floating-point values that represent the connection-strength weights between neurons in a neural network can be encoded directly into chromosomes in a genetic algorithm experiment. Figure 12.1 shows a recurrent network with 12 weights. If each weight is stored as a 32-bit floating-point number, we could represent all 12 weights as a single 12 * 32 = 384-bit chromosome. This is not a good representation scheme because connection weights usually are in the range (−10.0, +10.0), which is a very small percentage of the dynamic range of floating-point numbers. If we used this floating-point representation, a genetic algorithm would have to search a much larger space, with most of this space having essentially zero probability of containing a good set of connection weights to solve a given problem.

A better representation limits connection weights to the range (−10.0, +10.0) and encodes values in this range in a smaller number of bits. How many bits are required? It is important to not lose too much precision. In the next two sections, I design and implement an example program (with embedded C++ classes) that has the following behavior:

1. The number of bits used to store a weight is defined as a constant value.

2. A set of #define macros at the top of the program selects fitness functions for implementing single-bit rotation, the XOR problem, and the artificial life "smart" ant problem.

3. The packed weights in each chromosome are expanded into floating-point numbers to evaluate the "fitness" of a set of weights contained in a chromosome by simulating the control of an artificial ant in its environment.

4. The best chromosomes are propagated with genetic crossover and mutation to new generations.

5. Training time is very long compared to the backwards error propagation techniques used in Chapter 9. Genetic algorithm training makes sense for complex neural network architectures for which there is no (obvious) backwards error propagation procedure.

After experimenting with this example program, I reimplement it in Sec. 12.4 using a new procedure that I have developed (Copyright 1993 Mark Watson, all commercial rights reserved). This new example program (and embedded C++ classes) has the following behavior:

1. The number of bits used to store each weight is initially small.

2. After an initial training period, the number of bits used to encode weights is increased. This process is repeated until we have a high precision encoding of the weights (at least 12 to 14 bits per weight).

3. A set of #define macros at the top of the program selects fitness functions for implementing bit rotation, the XOR problem, and the artificial life "smart" ant problem.

4. The packed weights are expanded into floating-point numbers to evaluate the "fitness" of a set of weights contained in a chromosome by simulating the control of an artificial ant in its environment.

5. Training time is not as long as for the first example program. Genetic algorithm training makes sense for complex neural network architectures where there is no (obvious) backwards error propagation procedure.

In step 2, I initially have a smaller search space in which to find a population of weight sets to solve a problem. As an example, with the neural network shown in Figure 12.1, which contains 12 weights, I start by encoding 5 bits per weight, so that each chromosome in the population is initially only 60 bits long. After I find a good 60-bit chromosome population, I convert these weights to floating-point numbers and create a new population of chromosomes that encode 8-bit weights; now each chromosome in the population contains 96 bits. I continue this incremental search until each weight is represented by at least 12 bits.

In Sec. 12.4, I discuss how this incremental search, which I call VariGenSearch™, incrementally increases the dimensionality of the search space, but always begins the search with a set of good starting points (from the previous population, which uses lower-precision weights).

12.2 Test Problem Descriptions

I use three test problems to evaluate the utility of genetic neural network training:

1. Single-bit rotation

2. Boolean exclusive OR (XOR)

3. Artificial ant simulation

The first problem is trivial, and I use it to test simple neural network behavior quickly. The second problem is more difficult, and using a genetic algorithm can take many hours to train a network on a fast personal computer. In general, I would never use these genetic algorithm training procedures to solve the first two problems; the neural network C++ classes developed in Chapter 9 are much more efficient. The third problem demonstrates a better use of a hybrid genetic algorithm neural network program. A hybrid approach enables one to experiment with complex neural network topologies.

12.2.1 Single-bit rotation

Single-bit rotation is an easy learning problem for neural networks. Here is a simple example with a word four bits long:

```
input: 1000    output: 0100
input: 0100    output: 0010
input: 0010    output: 0001
input: 0001    output: 1000
```

I usually use this trivial learning example as a first test for all neural network simulation programs that I write.

12.2.2 Boolean exclusive OR (XOR)

XOR is a nontrivial learning problem for neural networks. Here is an example for a two-bit word:

```
input: 00    output: 0
input: 01    output: 1
input: 10    output: 1
input: 11    output: 0
```

12.2.3 Artificial ant simulation

The artificial ant has very simple behavior. It has two input sensors:

1. a sensor indicating that food is directly in front of it
2. a sensor indicating that it is blocked by a solid object

For both inputs, I represent a no-food or no-barrier condition by a negative input neuron value in the range (−0.2, −0.4) and the existence of food or a barrier with a positive value in the range (0.2, 0.4). For different problems, I usually experiment with both the range of input values and the output thresholds. The output threshold determines how I interpret the values of output neurons. I usually interpret negative output-neuron activation values as Boolean FALSE and positive values as Boolean TRUE.

The ant has three possible actions:

1. move forward one grid square
2. turn left
3. turn right

I represent the ant as a neural network with two input neurons and three output neurons. To control the ant, I repeat the following series of steps until the genetic algorithm's search has found a set of weights for a recurrent network that has "programmed" the ant to behave efficiently in its environment:

- for each chromosome in the population:
  - convert the chromosome into a set of floating-point weights
  - place the ant at the starting grid location
  - for N simulated time periods:
    - encode the ant's current environment into two values for the ant's input neurons
    - propagate the input values through the ant's neural network
    - find the maximum output neuron
    - perform one of the three ant actions based on which output neuron has the largest activation value
  - the ant's "fitness" function is a count of the number of pieces of food that it finds using a specified chromosome for its programming
- propagate the best chromosomes into the next generation using genetic crossover and mutation

The artificial ant needs a "playing field." In this simulation program, I provide an 8×8 grid with ant food placed along a trail. To make the problem more difficult, not every grid on this predefined trail has food on it. The ant has to learn a good strategy for finding the food trail when it encounters either a turn in the trail or a grid location on the trail that does not contain food. Figure 12.2 shows a sample 8×8 grid with a predefined trail.

The artificial ant needs to remember features of its environment that it has seen in the past; I use a recurrent network to provide this short-term memory. Figure 12.3 shows a network similar to that of Figure 12.1 that uses direct connections between the input and output neurons. The first experiments that I performed used the type of neural network shown in Figure 12.1 (same topology, with six hidden and three output neurons), but the ant was unable to learn complex behavior, since it did not have sufficient "short term" memory.

Before experimenting with the type of recurrent network shown in Figure 12.3, I anticipated that the ant would need to be able to remember more past actions and sensor input values. I had planned to provide more memory by modifying the type of

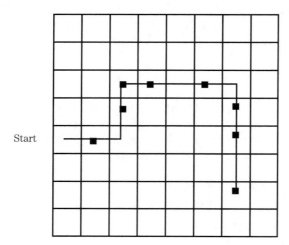

Figure 12.2 The artificial ant will learn to follow a food trail. Black dots along the train represent food.

network shown in Figure 12.3 by adding additional weights to connect the output of each output neuron back to the input of each input neuron; this new alternative design is shown in Figure 12.4.

The artificial ant uses a network with three output neurons and six hidden neurons. The network design is the same as in Figure 12.3, which is simplified by containing only two hidden and two output neurons.

If you experiment with the ant simulation program, adding to the environment, first try the network shown in Figure 12.3; if a longer short-term memory for recent events is necessary, add the output neuron layer to input neuron layer weights shown in Figure 12.4. A good alternative to Figure 12.4 is the addition of another hidden layer.

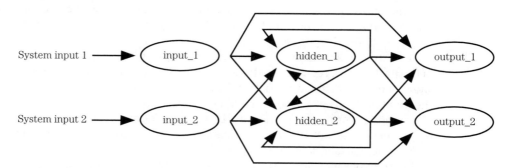

Figure 12.3 A recurrent neural network with two hidden-layer neurons whose outputs feed back to each neuron in the hidden layer (in addition to feeding forward to the output layer neurons). Additional weights directly connecting the input and output neurons increase the network's ability to remember previous sensor inputs. The example program uses this topology with two input, six hidden, and three output neurons.

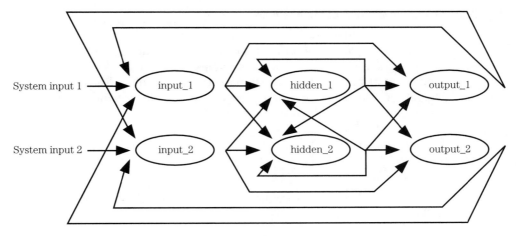

Figure 12.4   A recurrent network that feeds the output of every neuron to the input of every other neuron in the network. The example program does not require the extra weights connecting output back to input neurons to solve the ant problem.

12.3 Example Program Using Fixed-Size Weights

In Sec. 12.2.3, I presented the basic algorithm for training an ant to interact efficiently with its environment. The example program listed in this section is set up to solve all three problems described in Sec. 12.2.

The fundamental programming problem in the example program lies in the representation of weights as short bit strings. I need to string all the weights, in whatever representation I am using, into one long contiguous bit sequence. I will also make my programming job easier if I can reuse the bit-vector classes developed in Chapter 6.

12.3.1 Initial prototype

In my first prototype implementation (which is not listed in this chapter), I subclassed the bit-vector class to add the following new data and behavior:

1. Addition of a static member data element, which was one large contiguous bit vector

2. A class constructor allocated the data for new instances contiguously into the static bit vector

This implementation supported the creation of individual bit vectors, which were all stored in order in memory. This ordering allowed all bit vectors (each representing individual weight sets: input neuron layer to hidden neuron layer, etc.) to be treated as one large chromosome (bit vector) for purposes of implementing genetic learning.

This implementation had the advantage that the size of a neural network could be set dynamically in an executing program. The disadvantage was that the resulting implementation was fairly complex.

12.3.2 Final implementation of the example program

The final implementation of the example program is listed in this section. I have simplified the implementation by statistically allocating the two-dimensional connection-weight arrays. The dimension values are set using `const` definitions at the beginning of the program. To support genetic learning, I need to map a single-bit vector into the set of two-dimensional floating-point weight arrays. The size of the neural network is set by the `const` definitions:

```
const int NUM_INPUTS  = 4;
const int NUM_HIDDEN  = 5;
const int NUM_OUTPUTS = 4;
```

The topology of the neural network is determined by defining some or all of the following:

```
#define USE_I_TO_O // extra weights between input and output neurons
#define USE_H_TO_H // extra weights between hidden and hidden neurons
#define USE_O_TO_H // extra weights between output and hidden neurons
```

For example, the difference between the neural network topologies shown in Figures 12.1 and 12.3 is determined by these definitions.
To implement Figure 12.1, use the following definitions:

```
#define USE_H_TO_H // extra weights between hidden and hidden neurons
#define USE_O_TO_H // extra weights between output and hidden neurons
```

To implement Figure 12.3, use the following definitions:

```
#define USE_I_TO_O // extra weights between input and output neurons
#define USE_H_TO_H // extra weights between hidden and hidden neurons
#define USE_O_TO_H // extra weights between output and hidden neurons
```

Figure 12.5 shows the class diagram for class `genetic_recurrent_network`. An instance of this class contains static allocation of two-dimensional weight arrays and a set of single large bit vectors (chromosomes). The population is a set of these large single bit vectors. The public member function `copy_bit_weights_to_floats` unpacks the bit vector for a specified member of the chromosome population into the two-dimensional floating-point bit arrays. The genetic learning is implemented by genetic crossover and mutation on these bit vectors. The fitness member function evaluates each chromosome by using the two-dimensional weight arrays as temporary storage to implement a neural network for each member of the chromosome population. I reuse a single set of two-dimensional floating-point weight arrays to evaluate all chromosomes in the population.

The following listing shows the implementation of the `genetic_recurrent_net work` class, and the initialization and fitness functions for all three sample problems.

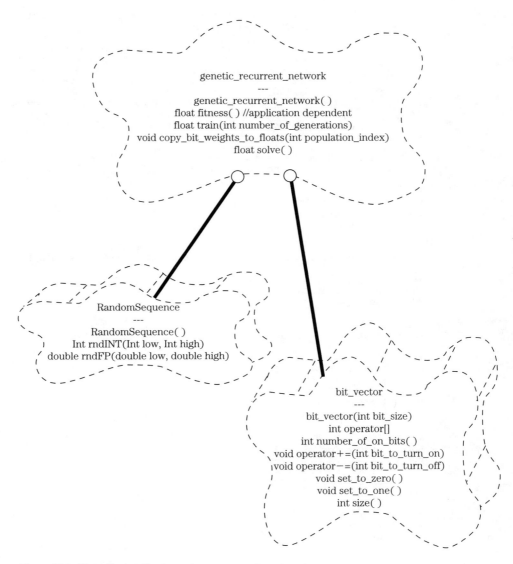

Figure 12.5 Class diagram for `genetic_recurrent_network`.

```
// File: fix_size.cp
//
// Description: This file contains the class definition for
//              genetic_recurrent_network, and the problem setup
//              and simulation code for all three problems in
//              Chapter 12:
//
//                   1. single bit rotation (easy neural network test problem)
```

```
//                     2. XOR (more difficult neural network test problem)
//                     3. Artificial ant simulation
//
//              As mentioned in the text, the first two problems are
//              solved better and faster by using the neural network
//              classes developed in Chapter 12. The third problem
//              requires a (highly) recurrent neural network (or its
//              equivalent) to solve; we use a genetic algorithm
//              to find a good set of weights to control ant behavior
//              out of the huge search space of all possible weight
//              values for the specified neural network architecture.
//
//
// This software may be used without restriction in compiled form.
// This source code may not be redistributed without permission.
//

#include "bit_vect.h"
#include "randseq.h"
#include <math.h>


// Three test problems: single bit rotation, XOR, and ant simulation

#define DO_XOR
//#define DO_ROTATION
//#define DO_ANT

const float MIN_VAL = -10.0;
const float MAX_VAL =  10.0;

#ifdef DO_XOR
const int NUM_INPUTS  = 2;
const int NUM_HIDDEN  = 6;
const int NUM_OUTPUTS = 1;
const int POPULATION = 500;
#endif

#ifdef DO_ROTATION
const int NUM_INPUTS  = 4;
const int NUM_HIDDEN  = 5;
const int NUM_OUTPUTS = 4;
const int POPULATION = 10;
#endif

#ifdef DO_ANT
const int NUM_INPUTS  = 2;
const int NUM_HIDDEN  = 6;
const int NUM_OUTPUTS = 3;
// comment out the following line for the network shown
// in Figure 12.3:
#define USE_I_TO_O
#define USE_H_TO_H
#define USE_O_TO_H
const int POPULATION = 50;
#endif


//
//              Function: sigmoid
//
//              See Figure 8.2
//
```

```
float sigmoid(float x)
{
    return (1.0 / (1.0 + exp(-x))) - 0.5;
}


class genetic_recurrent_network
{
 public:
    genetic_recurrent_network(int bits_per_value);
   ~genetic_recurrent_network();
    float fitness();  // for weights copied to float weight arrays
    float train(int number_of_generations); // return best fitness
    void copy_bit_weights_to_floats(int population_index);
    float solve();

 private:
    int bit_size;
    int int_range;
    int num_bits_per_chromosome;
    bit_vector **population;
    // float storage for weights (a chromosome with a specified
    // population index can be copied into these arrays to make
    // writing the fitness() function easier):
    float i_to_h[NUM_INPUTS][NUM_HIDDEN];
#ifdef USE_I_TO_O
    float i_to_o[NUM_INPUTS][NUM_OUTPUTS];
#endif
#ifdef USE_H_TO_H
    float h_to_h[NUM_HIDDEN][NUM_HIDDEN];
    float hidden_sums[NUM_HIDDEN];
#endif
#ifdef USE_O_TO_H
    float o_to_h[NUM_OUTPUTS][NUM_HIDDEN];
#endif
    float h_to_o[NUM_HIDDEN][NUM_OUTPUTS];

    float inputs[NUM_INPUTS];
    float hidden[NUM_HIDDEN];
    float outputs[NUM_OUTPUTS];

    void propagate();

    float *fitnesses;

    void initialize_population();
    void sort_by_fitness();

    RandomSequence ran_seq;
};

//
//          Data used to define 2 raised to the power N for n=0..15
//

static int powers_of_two[] = {1,2,4,8,16,32,64,128,256,512,1024,2048,
                              4096, 8192, 16384, 32768};

//
//          Class definition for genetic_recurrent_network
//

genetic_recurrent_network::genetic_recurrent_network(int bits_per_value)
```

```
{
    bit_size = bits_per_value;
    int_range = powers_of_two[bit_size];
    population = new bit_vector * [POPULATION];
    num_bits_per_chromosome =
        bit_size *(NUM_INPUTS*NUM_HIDDEN
#ifdef USE_H_TO_H
                + NUM_HIDDEN*NUM_HIDDEN
#endif
#ifdef USE_I_TO_O
                + NUM_INPUTS*NUM_OUTPUTS
#endif
#ifdef USE_O_TO_H
                + NUM_OUTPUTS*NUM_HIDDEN
#endif
                + NUM_HIDDEN*NUM_OUTPUTS);
    for (int i=0; i<POPULATION; i++)
        population[i] = new bit_vector(num_bits_per_chromosome);
    fitnesses = new float[POPULATION];

    initialize_population();
    for (i=0; i<POPULATION; i++)
    {
        copy_bit_weights_to_floats(i);
        fitnesses[i] = fitness();
    }
    sort_by_fitness();
}

//
//          Class destructor for genetic_recurrent_network
//

genetic_recurrent_network::~genetic_recurrent_network()
{
    delete [] population;
    delete [] fitnesses;
}

//
//          Member function copy_bits_to_floats
//
//          This function converts a specified chromosome (bit vector)
//          in the population to the floating-point weights.
//

void genetic_recurrent_network::copy_bit_weights_to_floats(int population_index)
{
    bit_vector *b = population[population_index];
    int start_bit = 0;
    int i, j, k, val;
    float f_val;

    // input to hidden weights:
    for (i=0; i<NUM_INPUTS; i++)
    {
        for (j=0; j<NUM_HIDDEN; j++)
        {
            val = 0;
            for (k=0; k<bit_size; k++)
                if ((*b)[k+start_bit])
                    val += powers_of_two[bit_size - k - 1];
            f_val = val;
            f_val = (f_val / ((float)int_range))
```

```
                             * (MAX_VAL - MIN_VAL) + MIN_VAL;
                start_bit += bit_size;
                i_to_h[i][j] = f_val;
            }
    }

#ifdef USE_I_TO_O

    // input to output weights:
    for (i=0; i<NUM_INPUTS; i++)
    {
        for (j=0; j<NUM_OUTPUTS; j++)
        {
            val = 0;
            for (k=0; k<bit_size; k++)
                if ((*b)[k+start_bit])
                    val += powers_of_two[bit_size - k - 1];
            f_val = val;
            f_val = (f_val / ((float)int_range))
                     * (MAX_VAL - MIN_VAL) + MIN_VAL;
            start_bit += bit_size;
            i_to_o[i][j] = f_val;
        }
    }

#endif

#ifdef USE_H_TO_H

    // hidden to hidden weights:
    for (i=0; i<NUM_HIDDEN; i++)
    {
        for (j=0; j<NUM_HIDDEN; j++)
        {
            val = 0;
            for (k=0; k<bit_size; k++)
                if ((*b)[k+start_bit])
                    val += powers_of_two[bit_size - k - 1];
            f_val = val;
            f_val = (f_val / ((float)int_range))
                     * (MAX_VAL - MIN_VAL) + MIN_VAL;
            start_bit += bit_size;
            h_to_h[i][j] = f_val;
        }
    }

#endif

#ifdef USE_O_TO_H

    // output to hidden weights:
    for (i=0; i<NUM_OUTPUTS; i++)
    {
        for (j=0; j<NUM_HIDDEN; j++)
        {
            val = 0;
            for (k=0; k<bit_size; k++)
                if ((*b)[k+start_bit])
                    val += powers_of_two[bit_size - k - 1];
            f_val = val;
            f_val = (f_val / ((float)int_range))
                     * (MAX_VAL - MIN_VAL) + MIN_VAL;
            start_bit += bit_size;
            o_to_h[i][j] = f_val;
```

```
            }
        }

#endif
    // hidden to output weights:
    for (i=0; i<NUM_HIDDEN; i++)
    {
        for (j=0; j<NUM_OUTPUTS; j++)
        {
            val = 0;
            for (k=0; k<bit_size; k++)
                if ((*b)[k+start_bit])
                    val += powers_of_two[bit_size - k - 1];
            f_val = val;
            f_val = (f_val / ((float)int_range))
                    * (MAX_VAL - MIN_VAL) + MIN_VAL;
            start_bit += bit_size;
            h_to_o[i][j] = f_val;
        }
    }
}

//
//          Member function initialize_population
//

void genetic_recurrent_network::initialize_population()
{
    for (int i=0; i<POPULATION; i++)
    {
        for (int j=0; j<num_bits_per_chromosome; j++)
        {
            int index = ran_seq.rndINT(0, num_bits_per_chromosome - 1);
            (*population[i]) += index;
        }
    }
}

//
//          Member function sort_by_fitness
//
//          Note: I use a "bubble sort" here.  This is not efficient
//                for very large populations as the sort time is
//                O(number of chromosomes squared)
//

void genetic_recurrent_network::sort_by_fitness()
{
    float x;
    bit_vector *b;
    for (int i=0; i<POPULATION; i++)
    {
        for (int j=(POPULATION - 2); j>=i; j--)
        {
            if (fitnesses[j] > fitnesses[j+1])
            {
                x = fitnesses[j];
                b = population[j];
                fitnesses[j] = fitnesses[j+1];
                population[j] = population[j+1];
                fitnesses[j+1] = x;
                population[j+1] = b;
            }
        }
    }
```

```
    }
#if 0
    cerr << "fitnesses: ";
    for (i=0; i<POPULATION; i++) cerr << fitnesses[i] << " ";
    cerr << "\n";
#endif
}

//
//          Member function solve
//
//          This function modifies the population with genetic
//          crossovers and mutation. It then uses the application-
//          specific fitness function to rate the fitness of each
//          chromosome in the new population.
//

float genetic_recurrent_network::solve()
{
    int i = 0, j;
    for (j=3*POPULATION/4 + 1; j<POPULATION; j++)
    {   // copy chromosome # i to # j:
        for (int k=0; k<num_bits_per_chromosome; k++)
        {
            if ((*population[i])[k])
                (*population[j]) += k;
            else
                (*population[j]) -= k;
        }
        i++;
        if (i >= (POPULATION/4 + 1))  i = 0;
    }

    // crossovers:
    for (j=0; j<POPULATION/5; j++)
    {
        int chrom_1 = ran_seq.rndINT(POPULATION/10+1, POPULATION - 1);
        int chrom_2 = ran_seq.rndINT(POPULATION/10+1, POPULATION - 1);
        int crossover_location =
            ran_seq.rndINT(1,num_bits_per_chromosome/bit_size);
        crossover_location *= bit_size;
        for (int k=0; k<crossover_location; k++)
        {
            int save = (*population[chrom_2])[k];
            if ((*population[chrom_1])[k])
                (*population[chrom_2]) += k;
            else
                (*population[chrom_2]) -= k;
            if (save)
                (*population[chrom_1]) += k;
            else
                (*population[chrom_1]) -= k;
        }
        i++;
    }

    // mutations:

    for (j=5; j<POPULATION; j++)
    {
        if (ran_seq.rndFP(0.0, 100.0) < 10.0)
        {
            int location = ran_seq.rndINT(0, num_bits_per_chromosome - 1);
            if ((*population[j])[location])
```

```
                                    (*population[j]) -= location;
                      else
                                    (*population[j]) += location;
            }
    }

    // very high mutations for 1/8 of the population:

    for (j=7*POPULATION/8; j<POPULATION; j++)
    {
            for (int m=0; m<num_bits_per_chromosome/4+2; m++)
            {
                    if (ran_seq.rndFP(0.0, 100.0) < 75.0)
                    {
                            int location = ran_seq.rndINT(0, num_bits_per_chromosome - 1);
                            if ((*population[j])[location])
                                    (*population[j]) -= location;
                            else
                                    (*population[j]) += location;
                    }
            }
    }

    // Heuristic: I have noticed that sometimes there is a block
    // of highly rated (by the fitness function), identical
    // chromosomes at the beginning of the population list. The
    // following check simply mutates any identical chromosomes
    // so that we do not waste time evaluating identical members
    // of the population:

    for (i=0; i<POPULATION-1; i++)
    {
            for (j=i+1; j<POPULATION; j++)
            {
                    if ((*population[i]) == ((*population[j])))
                    {
                            int mutation_location =
                                    ran_seq.rndINT(0, num_bits_per_chromosome - 1);
                            if ((*population[j])[mutation_location])
                                    (*population[j]) -= mutation_location;
                            else
                                    (*population[j]) += mutation_location;
                    }
            }
    }

    // Evaluate the fitness values of all chromosomes in the population:
    for (i=0; i<POPULATION; i++)
    {
            copy_bit_weights_to_floats(i);
            fitnesses[i] = fitness();
    }
    sort_by_fitness();

    // DEBUG printout:
#if 0
    for (i=0; i<POPULATION; i++)
    {
            cerr << "\nchrom: ";
            for (j=0; j<num_bits_per_chromosome; j++)
                    cerr << (*population[i])[j] << " ";
    }
    cerr << "\n";
#endif
```

```
        return fitnesses[0];
}

//
//              Member function propagate
//
//              This function does not directly use any chromosomes
//              in the current population.  It is used to propagate the
//              current input-neuron activation values through the network
//              using the current weight set (as defined by member function
//              copy_bit_weights_to_floats for a specified chromosome).
//

void genetic_recurrent_network::propagate()
{
    for (int h=0; h<NUM_HIDDEN; h++)
    {
        hidden[h] = 0.0;
#ifdef USE_H_TO_H
        hidden_sums[h] = 0.0;
#endif
    }

#ifdef USE_H_TO_H
    for (int cycle=0; cycle<3; cycle++)
#endif
    {
        for (h=0; h<NUM_HIDDEN; h++)
        {
            for (int i=0; i<NUM_INPUTS; i++)
            {
                hidden[h] += inputs[i] * i_to_h[i][h];
            }
#ifdef USE_H_TO_H
            for (int h2=0; h2<NUM_HIDDEN; h2++)
            {
                hidden_sums[h] += hidden[h2] * h_to_h[h2][h];
            }
#endif
#ifdef USE_O_TO_H
            for (int o2=0; o2<NUM_OUTPUTS; o2++)
            {
                hidden_sums[h] += outputs[o2] * o_to_h[o2][h];
            }
#endif

#ifndef USE_H_TO_H
            hidden[h] = sigmoid(hidden[h]);
#else
            hidden[h] = sigmoid(hidden_sums[h]);
#endif
        }

        for (int o=0; o<NUM_OUTPUTS; o++)
            outputs[o] = 0.0;
        for (o=0; o<NUM_OUTPUTS; o++)
        {
            for (h=0; h<NUM_HIDDEN; h++)
            {
                outputs[o] += hidden[h] * h_to_o[h][o];
            }

#ifdef USE_I_TO_O
            for (int i=0; i<NUM_INPUTS; i++)
```

```
                           {
                               outputs[o] += inputs[i] * i_to_o[i][o];
                           }
#endif
               }
           for (o=0; o<NUM_OUTPUTS; o++)
           {
               outputs[o] = sigmoid(outputs[o]);
           }
       }
}


//
//          Member function train
//
//          This function creates a specific number of new
//          generations in the population and uses member
//          function solve to evaluate each chromosome in each
//          population.
//

float genetic_recurrent_network::train(int num_generations)
{
    float best_error;
    for (int i=0; i<num_generations; i++)
    {
        best_error = solve();
        cerr << "current best error =" << best_error << "\n";
    }
    return best_error;
}


// APPLICATION-SPECIFIC FITNESS FUNCTION:

inline float val_sq(float x)
{
    return x * x;
}

int debug = 0;

#ifdef DO_ROTATION
float genetic_recurrent_network::fitness()
{
    static float in_1[]   = { 0.2, -0.2, -0.2, -0.2};
    static float in_2[]   = {-0.2,  0.2, -0.2, -0.2};
    static float in_3[]   = {-0.2, -0.2,  0.2, -0.2};
    static float in_4[]   = {-0.2, -0.2, -0.2,  0.2};
    static float out_1[]  = {-0.2, -0.2, -0.2,  0.2};
    static float out_2[]  = { 0.2, -0.2, -0.2, -0.2};
    static float out_3[]  = {-0.2,  0.2, -0.2, -0.2};
    static float out_4[]  = {-0.2, -0.2,  0.2, -0.2};

    float error = 0.0;
    for (int i=0; i<4; i++)
    {
        inputs[0] = in_1[i];
        inputs[1] = in_2[i];
        inputs[2] = in_3[i];
        inputs[3] = in_4[i];
        propagate();
        error += val_sq(outputs[0] - out_1[i]);
        error += val_sq(outputs[1] - out_2[i]);
```

```
            error += val_sq(outputs[2] - out_3[i]);
            error += val_sq(outputs[3] - out_4[i]);
            if (debug)
            {
                cerr << "inputs: " << inputs[0] << ", " << inputs[1]
                     << ", " << inputs[2] << ", " << inputs[3]
                     << "  outputs: " << outputs[0] << ", " << outputs[1]
                     << ", " << outputs[2] << ", " << outputs[3] << "\n";
            }
        }
 //     cerr << "RMS error =" << error << "\n";
        return sqrt(error);
}
#endif


#ifdef DO_XOR

//                  XOR test problem setup:

float genetic_recurrent_network::fitness()
{
    // test with a fitness for XOR function:
    static float in_1[] = {-0.21, -0.2,   0.2,    0.2};
    static float in_2[] = {-0.2,   0.22, -0.2,    0.2};
    static float out[]  = {-0.201, 0.21,  0.19, -0.192};

    float error = 0.0;
    for (int i=0; i<4; i++)
    {
        inputs[0] = in_1[i];
        inputs[1] = in_2[i];
        propagate();
        error += val_sq(outputs[0] - out[i]);
        if (debug)
        {
            cerr << "inputs: " << inputs[0] << ", " << inputs[1]
                 << "  output: " << outputs[0] << "\n";
        }
    }
 //     cerr << "RMS error =" << error << "\n";
    return sqrt(error);
}
#endif


#ifdef DO_ANT

const int NUM_ANT_CYCLES = 30;

float genetic_recurrent_network::fitness()
{

    float error = 8;  // represents eight uneaten pieces of ant food

    // Initial environment for the ant:
    int current_x = 0; // ant's starting grid position
    int current_y = 3;

    // direction values: 1=up, 2=right, 3=down, 4=left
    // (looking at Figure 12.3)
    int current_direction = 2;

    int grid[8][8];
```

```
for (int i=0; i<8; i++)
    for (int j=0; j<8; j++)
        grid[i][j] = 0;
// Initial ant food locations on the grid:
grid[1][3] = grid[2][4] = grid[2][5] = grid[3][5] = 1;
grid[5][5] = grid[6][4] = grid[6][3] = grid[6][1] = 1;

// Initial sensor values:
inputs[0] =  0.3; // food in the square in front of the ant
inputs[1] = -0.3; // no wall in front of the ant

int eating_flag = 0;

// Output codes:
//
//     Highest output neuron     meaning
//     ---------------------     -------
//
//                         0     move forward
//                         1     turn to the left
//                         2     turn to the right
//

for (i=0; i<NUM_ANT_CYCLES; i++)
{
    eating_flag = 0;
    propagate();
    // Find the largest output-neuron value:
    int max_index = 0;
    float max_val = outputs[0];
    for (int m=1; m<NUM_OUTPUTS; m++)
    {
        if (max_val < outputs[m])
        {
            max_val = outputs[m];
            max_index = m;
        }
    }

    switch (max_index)
    {
        case 0:   // move forward
            switch(current_direction)
            {
                case 1:  // up (y coordinate increases)
                    if (current_y <= 6)  current_y++;
                    break;
                case 2:  // right (x coordinate increases)
                    if (current_x <= 6)  current_x++;
                    break;
                case 3:  // down (y coordiante decreases)
                    if (current_y > 0)  current_y--;
                    break;
                case 4:  // left (x coordinate decreases)
                    if (current_x > 0) current_x--;
                    break;
            }
            if (grid[current_x][current_y] != 0)
            {
                error -= 1;
                grid[current_x][current_y] = 0; // cannot eat food twice!
                if (debug)
                {
                    eating_flag = 1;
```

```
                    }
                }
                break;
            case 1: // turn left
                current_direction -= 1;
                if (current_direction < 1) current_direction = 1;
                break;
            case 2: // turn right
                current_direction  += 1;
                if (current_direction > 4) current_direction = 4;
                break;
        }

#ifdef DEBUG
        if (debug)
        {
            cerr << "in: " << inputs[0] << ", " << inputs[1]
                 << "  out: " << outputs[0] << ", " << outputs[1]
                 << ", " << outputs[2] << "\n";
        }
#endif

        // Set input-neuron sensors for the next iteration:

        inputs[0] = inputs[1] = -0.3;
        int next_x = current_x;
        int next_y = current_y;
        switch (current_direction)
        {
            case 1: // up
                if (current_y <= 6)
                {
                    next_y += 1;
                } else
                {
                    inputs[1] = +0.3; // path blocked by boundary
                }
                break;
            case 2: // right
                if (current_x <= 6)
                {
                    next_x += 1;
                } else
                {
                    inputs[1] = +0.3; // path blocked by boundary
                }
                break;
            case 3: // down
                if (current_y >= 1)
                {
                    next_y -= 1;
                } else
                {
                    inputs[1] = +0.3; // path blocked by boundary
                }
                break;
            case 4: // left
                if (current_x >= 1)
                {
                    next_x -= 1;
                } else
                {
                    inputs[1] = +0.3; // path blocked by boundary
                }
```

```
                            break;
                    }
                    if (grid[next_x][next_y] != 0)
                        inputs[0] = +0.3; // food directly in front of the ant
                    if (debug)
                    {
                        if (eating_flag == 0)
                            cerr << "  (" << current_x << ", " << current_y << ")    ";
                        else
                            cerr << " <[" << current_x << ", " << current_y << "]>  ";
                        if (((i+1)/5)*5 == (i+1))  cerr << "\n";
                    }

                }
                if (debug)  cerr << "\n\n";

    //    cerr << "RMS error =" << error << "\n";
                return error;
        }
        #endif

        void main()
        {
            genetic_recurrent_network v2(12);
            cerr << "Starting...\n";
            for (int iter=0; iter<10000; iter++)
            {
                debug = 0;
                v2.train(5);
                debug = 1;
                v2.copy_bit_weights_to_floats(0); //should be the best one!
                cerr << "\n\ngeneration " << 5*(iter + 1) << "\n";
                v2.fitness();
            }
        }
```

12.3.3 Example execution for the bit-rotation problem

The single-bit rotation problem serves as a simple test of genetic learning of neural network weight sets. In the following listings, the neural network inputs and generated outputs, from the weights for the "best" chromosome in the current generation, are shown for a series of generations.

```
generation 15
inputs:  0.2, -0.2, -0.2, -0.2  outputs: -0.227343,  0.477713, -0.494209, -0.107122
inputs: -0.2,  0.2, -0.2, -0.2  outputs: -0.432832, -0.273418,  0.392323, -0.182954
inputs: -0.2, -0.2,  0.2, -0.2  outputs: -0.364282,  0.034837, -0.398906, 0.434958
inputs: -0.2, -0.2, -0.2,  0.2  outputs: 0.431719, -0.047936, 0.48531, 0.039318
current best error =1.024979
current best error =1.024979


generation 210
inputs: 0.2, -0.2, -0.2, -0.2  outputs: -0.118767, 0.474425, -0.065722, -0.114854
inputs: -0.2, 0.2, -0.2, -0.2  outputs: -0.40837, -0.266388, 0.113176, -0.199201
inputs: -0.2, -0.2, 0.2, -0.2  outputs: -0.257627, -0.138141, -0.016848, 0.423016
inputs: -0.2, -0.2, -0.2, 0.2  outputs: 0.340571, -0.285315, -0.094627, 0.000956

current best error =0.575766
current best error =0.575766
current best error =0.575766
```

```
current best error =0.228026
current best error =0.228026


generation 4625
inputs: 0.2, -0.2, -0.2, -0.2  outputs: -0.25088, 0.388767, -0.241641, -0.149191
inputs: -0.2, 0.2, -0.2, -0.2  outputs: -0.233142, -0.161311, 0.19184, -0.146711
inputs: -0.2, -0.2, 0.2, -0.2  outputs: -0.1915, -0.23533, -0.198328, 0.186456
inputs: -0.2, -0.2, -0.2, 0.2  outputs: 0.212441, -0.18896, -0.217967, -0.156974
```

12.3.4 Example execution for the XOR problem

The following listing shows the start of an XOR genetic training experiment.

```
Starting...
current best error =0.394889
current best error =0.383791
current best error =0.383791
current best error =0.382181
current best error =0.382181


generation 5
inputs: -0.21, -0.2  output: 0.044284
inputs: -0.2, 0.22  output: 0.070185
inputs: 0.2, -0.2  output: -0.020223
inputs: 0.2, 0.2  output: -0.043149
```

Here, after only five generations, the error is still large, and the best set of neural network weights in the chromosome population cannot solve the XOR problem.

```
current best error =0.369644
current best error =0.369562

generation 60
inputs: -0.21, -0.2  output: -0.014189
inputs: -0.2, 0.22  output: 0.034584
inputs: 0.2, -0.2  output: 0.01126
inputs: 0.2, 0.2  output: 0.00538
current best error =0.369477
current best error =0.369477
current best error =0.369477
```

In this listing the error is smaller, but the best set of weights in the chromosome population still has not learned to map (TRUE, TRUE) into (FALSE).

```
current best error =0.350609
current best error =0.350609


generation 350
inputs: -0.21, -0.2  output: -0.023129
inputs: -0.2, 0.22  output: 0.045854
inputs: 0.2, -0.2  output: 0.021295
inputs: 0.2, 0.2  output: -0.002572
current best error =0.350609
current best error =0.350609
current best error =0.350608
```

The next listing shows that the best set of weights after 1240 generations has improved very little. Again, this example shows that I only want to use genetic algorithm learning of neural network weights when I require highly recurrent networks.

```
current best error =0.350527
current best error =0.350524


generation 1240
inputs: -0.21, -0.2  output: -0.022586
inputs: -0.2, 0.22  output: 0.046483
inputs: 0.2, -0.2  output: 0.020841
inputs: 0.2, 0.2  output: -0.003101
current best error =0.350524
current best error =0.350524
```

Even though the error is still large, the network using the best set of weights in the chromosome population can distinguish all cases of the XOR problem if I apply a hard threshold: interpret any output value greater than zero as a Boolean TRUE value, and any output less than zero as a Boolean FALSE value.

In the next section, I present a more appropriate use of genetic algorithm learning for discovering good sets of neural network weights.

12.3.5 Example execution for the artificial ant problem

The following output shows the simulation with 100 chromosomes in the population. Coordinates bracketed with <[ ]> indicate locations that contained food (which the ant eats immediately).

```
generation 5
 <[1, 3]>      (2, 3)       (2, 3)     <[2, 4]>      (2, 4)
  (3, 4)       (3, 4)     <[3, 5]>      (3, 6)       (3, 6)
  (3, 6)       (3, 6)       (3, 6)      (3, 6)       (3, 6)
  (3, 6)       (3, 7)       (3, 7)      (3, 7)       (3, 7)
  (3, 7)       (3, 7)       (3, 7)      (3, 7)       (3, 7)
  (3, 7)       (3, 7)       (3, 7)      (3, 7)       (3, 7)
```

Note that after five generations, the ant is still getting "stuck" at the edge of the grid. Three out of eight pieces of food have been eaten. Figure 12.6 shows the path taken by an ant using the best set of weights found after five generations.

```
generation 15
 <[1, 3]>      (1, 3)       (1, 3)      (1, 3)       (1, 4)
  (1, 4)       (1, 4)     <[2, 4]>      (2, 4)     <[2, 5]>
  (2, 5)       (2, 5)     <[3, 5]>      (3, 5)       (3, 5)
  (3, 5)       (3, 6)       (3, 6)      (3, 6)       (3, 6)
  (3, 7)       (3, 7)       (3, 7)      (3, 7)       (3, 7)
  (3, 7)       (3, 7)       (3, 7)      (3, 7)       (3, 7)
```

After fifteen generations, the ant still gets stuck at an edge, but manages to eat four out of eight pieces of food before getting stuck.

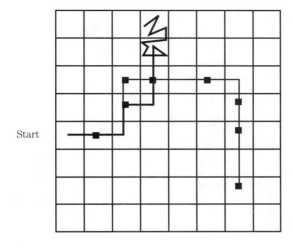

Figure 12.6 The ant has not learned to deal with its environment after only five generations. The ant's trail is represented by a thick line. The food trail is represented by a thin line. Black dots represent food. In squares (3,6) and (3,7) the ant just wastes time by continually turning around, which I represent by a random path inside the grids (3,6) and (3,7).

Start

```
generation 25
 <[1, 3]>     (1, 3)      (1, 3)      (2, 3)      (2, 3)
 <[2, 4]>    <[2, 5]>     (2, 5)     <[3, 5]>     (3, 5)
  (3, 5)      (4, 5)     <[5, 5]>     (5, 5)      (5, 5)
  (6, 5)      (6, 5)      (6, 6)      (6, 6)      (6, 7)
  (6, 7)      (6, 7)      (6, 7)      (6, 7)      (6, 7)
  (6, 7)      (6, 7)      (6, 7)      (6, 7)      (6, 7)
```

After twenty five generations, the ant still gets stuck at an edge, but finds five pieces of food.

```
generation 30
 <[1, 3]>     (2, 3)      (3, 3)      (3, 3)      (3, 4)
 <[3, 5]>     (3, 6)      (3, 7)      (3, 7)      (4, 7)
  (5, 7)      (5, 7)      (5, 6)     <[5, 5]>     (5, 4)
  (5, 3)      (5, 3)     <[6, 3]>     (7, 3)      (7, 3)
  (7, 2)      (7, 1)      (7, 1)     <[6, 1]>     (5, 1)
  (4, 1)      (4, 1)      (4, 0)      (4, 0)      (3, 0)
```

Figure 12.7 shows the behavior of the ant using the best set of weights found in thirty generations.

After thirty generations the ant seems to have learned not to get stuck. It also found five out of eight pieces of food on the grid.

```
generation 40
 <[1, 3]>     (1, 3)      (1, 3)      (2, 3)      (2, 3)
  (2, 3)      (2, 3)     <[2, 4]>    <[2, 5]>     (2, 5)
 <[3, 5]>     (3, 5)      (3, 5)      (4, 5)     <[5, 5]>
  (5, 5)      (5, 5)      (6, 5)      (6, 5)     <[6, 4]>
 <[6, 3]>     (6, 3)      (6, 3)      (6, 2)     <[6, 1]>
  (6, 1)      (6, 1)      (6, 0)      (6, 0)      (6, 0)
```

After forty generations, the ant once again gets stuck, but not until it finds all eight pieces of food. Figure 12.8 shows the ant's trail after forty generations.

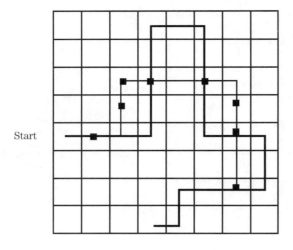

Figure 12.7 The artificial ant will learn to follow a food trail. Black dots along the trail represent food.

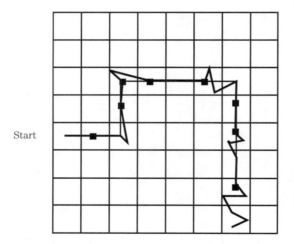

Figure 12.8 The ant's trail after forty generations. All eight pieces of food have been found. The ant has learned to turn in place to test the squares to the left and right for food if there is no food in the square that it is facing.

12.4 Example Program Using Variable Size Chromosomes Weights

Figure 12.9 shows the class diagram for `var_genetic_recurrent_network`.

The following listing shows the complete implementation of the C++ class `var_genetic_recurrent_network` and the solution to the three sample programs shown in this chapter. This example program is derived from the previous example; the class `genetic_recurrent_network` is renamed to `var_genetic_recurrent_network`, and the following member functions added to class `var_recurrent_network`:

- `copy_bit_weights_to_floats`
- `change_chromosome_size`

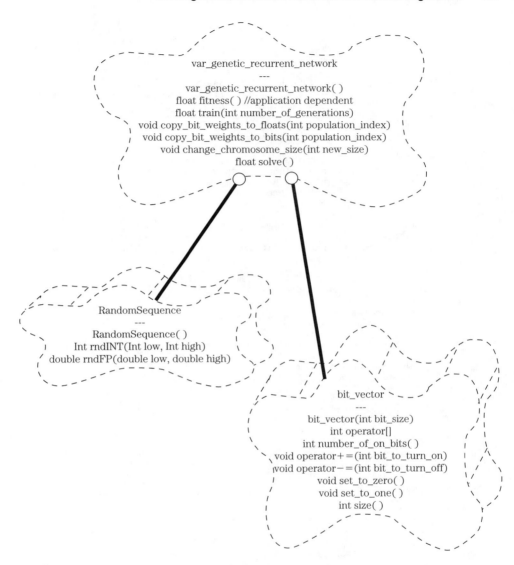

Figure 12.9 Class diagram for `var_genetic_recurrent_network`.

The following member function has been modified:

- `copy_bit_weights_to_floats`

Please note: unlike all other example programs in this book, use of the following program and the VariGenSearch™ algorithm is restricted to noncommercial applications unless written permission is obtained from the author.

```
// File: var_size.cp
//
```

```
// Description: This file contains the class definition for
//              var_genetic_recurrent_network, and the problem setup
//              and simulation code for all three problems in
//              Chapter 12:
//
//                 1. single-bit rotation (easy neural network test problem)
//                 2. XOR (more difficult neural network test problem)
//                 3. artificial ant simulation
//
//              As mentioned in the text, the first two problems are
//              solved better and faster by using the neural network
//              classes developed in Chapter 12. The third problem
//              requires a (highly) recurrent neural network (or its
//              equivalent) to solve; we use a genetic algorithm
//              to find a good set of weights to control ant behavior
//              out of the huge search space of all possible weight
//              values for the specified neural network architecture.
//
//
// This software may be used without restriction in compiled form
// for noncommercial applications. This source code may not be redistributed
// without permission.
//

#include "bit_vect.h"
#include "randseq.h"
#include <math.h>


// Three test problems: single-bit rotation, XOR, and ant simulation

//#define DO_ROTATION
//#define DO_XOR
#define DO_ANT

const float MIN_VAL = -10.0;
const float MAX_VAL =  10.0;

#ifdef DO_ROTATION
const int NUM_INPUTS  = 4;
const int NUM_HIDDEN  = 5;
const int NUM_OUTPUTS = 4;
const int POPULATION = 10;
#endif
#ifdef DO_XOR
const int NUM_INPUTS  = 2;
const int NUM_HIDDEN  = 3;
const int NUM_OUTPUTS = 1;
const int POPULATION = 500;
#endif

#ifdef DO_ANT
const int NUM_INPUTS  = 2;
const int NUM_HIDDEN  = 6;
const int NUM_OUTPUTS = 3;
// comment out the following line for the network shown
// in Figure 12.3:
#define USE_I_TO_O
#define USE_H_TO_H
#define USE_O_TO_H
const int POPULATION = 50;
#endif

//
```

```
//              Function: sigmoid
//
//              See Figure 8.2
//

float sigmoid(float x)
{
    return (1.0 / (1.0 + exp(-x))) - 0.5;
}


class var_genetic_recurrent_network
{
 public:
    var_genetic_recurrent_network(int bits_per_value);
   ~var_genetic_recurrent_network();
    float fitness();  // for weights copied to float weight arrays
    float train(int number_of_generations); // return best fitness
    void copy_bit_weights_to_floats(int population_index);
    void copy_float_weights_to_bits(int population_index);
    void change_chromosome_size(int new_size);
    float solve();

 private:
    int bit_size;
    int int_range;
    int num_bits_per_chromosome;
    bit_vector **population;

    // float storage for weights (a chromosome with a specified
    // population index can be copied into these arrays to make
    // writing the fitness() function easier):

    float i_to_h[NUM_INPUTS][NUM_HIDDEN];
#ifdef USE_I_TO_O
    float i_to_o[NUM_INPUTS][NUM_OUTPUTS];
#endif
#ifdef USE_H_TO_H
    float h_to_h[NUM_HIDDEN][NUM_HIDDEN];
    float hidden_sums[NUM_HIDDEN];
#endif
#ifdef USE_O_TO_H
    float o_to_h[NUM_OUTPUTS][NUM_HIDDEN];
#endif
    float h_to_o[NUM_HIDDEN][NUM_OUTPUTS];

    float inputs[NUM_INPUTS];
    float hidden[NUM_HIDDEN];
    float outputs[NUM_OUTPUTS];

    void propagate();

    float *fitnesses;

    void initialize_population();
    void sort_by_fitness();

    RandomSequence ran_seq;
};


//
//              Data used to define 2 raised to the power N for n=0..15
//
```

```
static int powers_of_two[] =
{1,2,4,8,16,32,64,128,256,512,1024,2048,4096, 8192, 16384, 32768};

//
//          Class definition for var_genetic_recurrent_network
//

var_genetic_recurrent_network::var_genetic_recurrent_network(int bits_per_value)
{
    bit_size = bits_per_value;
    int_range = powers_of_two[bit_size];
    population = new bit_vector * [POPULATION];
    num_bits_per_chromosome =
        bit_size *(NUM_INPUTS*NUM_HIDDEN
#ifdef USE_H_TO_H
                 + NUM_HIDDEN*NUM_HIDDEN
#endif
#ifdef USE_I_TO_O
                 + NUM_INPUTS*NUM_OUTPUTS
#endif
#ifdef USE_O_TO_H
                 + NUM_OUTPUTS*NUM_HIDDEN
#endif
                 + NUM_HIDDEN*NUM_OUTPUTS);
    for (int i=0; i<POPULATION; i++)
        population[i] = new bit_vector(num_bits_per_chromosome);
    fitnesses = new float[POPULATION];

    initialize_population();
    for (i=0; i<POPULATION; i++)
    {
        copy_bit_weights_to_floats(i);
        fitnesses[i] = fitness();
    }
    sort_by_fitness();
}


//
//          Member function change_chromosome_size
//

void var_genetic_recurrent_network::change_chromosome_size(int bits_per_value)
{
    // We need to copy the best 25% of the previous population into
    // a vector of floating point values:

    int num_floats =
                 NUM_INPUTS*NUM_HIDDEN
#ifdef USE_H_TO_H
                 + NUM_HIDDEN*NUM_HIDDEN
#endif
#ifdef USE_I_TO_O
                 + NUM_INPUTS*NUM_OUTPUTS
#endif
#ifdef USE_O_TO_H
                 + NUM_OUTPUTS*NUM_HIDDEN
#endif
                 + NUM_HIDDEN*NUM_OUTPUTS;
    int num_pop = (float)POPULATION * 0.25;

    num_floats *= num_pop;

    float *fp = new float[num_floats];
```

```
    int i, j, count = 0;
    for (int n=0; n<NUM_pop; n++)
    {
        copy_bit_weights_to_floats(n);
        for (i=0; i<NUM_INPUTS; i++)
        {
            for (j=0; j<NUM_HIDDEN; j++)
            {
                fp[count++] = i_to_h[i][j];
            }
        }
#ifdef USE_H_TO_H
        for (i=0; i<NUM_HIDDEN; i++)
        {
            for (j=0; j<NUM_HIDDEN; j++)
            {
                fp[count++] = h_to_h[i][j];
            }
        }

#endif
#ifdef USE_I_TO_O
        for (i=0; i<NUM_INPUTS; i++)
        {
            for (j=0; j<NUM_OUTPUTS; j++)
            {
                fp[count++] = i_to_o[i][j];
            }
        }

#endif
#ifdef USE_O_TO_H
        for (i=0; i<NUM_OUTPUTS; i++)
        {
            for (j=0; j<NUM_HIDDEN; j++)
            {
                fp[count++] = o_to_h[i][j];
            }
        }

#endif
        for (i=0; i<NUM_HIDDEN; i++)
        {
            for (j=0; j<NUM_OUTPUTS; j++)
            {
                fp[count++] = h_to_o[i][j];
            }
        }
    }


    // free the storage for the old population of chromosomes (bit vectors):
    delete [] population;

    bit_size = bits_per_value;
    int_range = powers_of_two[bit_size];
    population = new bit_vector * [POPULATION];
    num_bits_per_chromosome =
        bit_size *(NUM_INPUTS*NUM_HIDDEN
#ifdef USE_H_TO_H
            + NUM_HIDDEN*NUM_HIDDEN
#endif
#ifdef USE_I_TO_O
            + NUM_INPUTS*NUM_OUTPUTS
```

```
#endif
#ifdef USE_O_TO_H
                  + NUM_OUTPUTS*NUM_HIDDEN
#endif
                  + NUM_HIDDEN*NUM_OUTPUTS);
    for (i=0; i<POPULATION; i++)
        population[i] = new bit_vector(num_bits_per_chromosome);

    initialize_population();

    count = 0;
    for (n=0; n<NUM_pop; n++)
    {
        for (i=0; i<NUM_INPUTS; i++)
        {
            for (j=0; j<NUM_HIDDEN; j++)
            {
                i_to_h[i][j] = fp[count++];
            }
        }
#ifdef USE_H_TO_H
        for (i=0; i<NUM_HIDDEN; i++)
        {
            for (j=0; j<NUM_HIDDEN; j++)
            {
                h_to_h[i][j] = fp[count++];
            }
        }
#endif
#ifdef USE_I_TO_O
        for (i=0; i<NUM_INPUTS; i++)
        {
            for (j=0; j<NUM_OUTPUTS; j++)
            {
                i_to_o[i][j] = fp[count++];
            }
        }

#endif
#ifdef USE_O_TO_H
        for (i=0; i<NUM_OUTPUTS; i++)
        {
            for (j=0; j<NUM_HIDDEN; j++)
            {
                o_to_h[i][j] = fp[count++];
            }
        }

#endif
        for (i=0; i<NUM_HIDDEN; i++)
        {
            for (j=0; j<NUM_OUTPUTS; j++)
            {
                h_to_o[i][j] = fp[count++];
            }
        }
        copy_float_weights_to_bits(n);
    }

    delete [] fp;

    for (i=0; i<POPULATION; i++)
    {
        copy_bit_weights_to_floats(i);
```

```
        fitnesses[i] = fitness();
    }
    sort_by_fitness();
}


//
//          Class destructor for var_genetic_recurrent_network
//

var_genetic_recurrent_network::~var_genetic_recurrent_network()
{
    delete [] population;
    delete [] fitnesses;
}


//
//          Member function copy_bit_weights_to_floats
//
//          This function converts a specified chromosome (bit vector)
//          in the population to the floating-point weights.
//

void var_genetic_recurrent_network::
          copy_bit_weights_to_floats(int population_index)
{
    bit_vector *b = population[population_index];
    int start_bit = 0;
    int i, j, k, val;
    float f_val;

    // input to hidden weights:
    for (i=0; i<NUM_INPUTS; i++)
    {
        for (j=0; j<NUM_HIDDEN; j++)
        {
            val = 0;
            for (k=0; k<bit_size; k++)
                if ((*b)[k+start_bit])
                    val += powers_of_two[bit_size - k - 1];
            f_val = val;
            f_val = (f_val / ((float)int_range))
                  * (MAX_VAL - MIN_VAL) + MIN_VAL;
            start_bit += bit_size;
            i_to_h[i][j] = f_val;
        }
    }

#ifdef USE_I_TO_O

    // input to output weights:
    for (i=0; i<NUM_INPUTS; i++)
    {
        for (j=0; j<NUM_OUTPUTS; j++)
        {
            val = 0;
            for (k=0; k<bit_size; k++)
                if ((*b)[k+start_bit])
                    val += powers_of_two[bit_size - k - 1];
            f_val = val;
            f_val = (f_val / ((float)int_range))
                  * (MAX_VAL - MIN_VAL) + MIN_VAL;
            start_bit += bit_size;
            i_to_o[i][j] = f_val;
        }
```

```
        }

#endif

#ifdef USE_H_TO_H

    // hidden to hidden weights:
    for (i=0; i<NUM_HIDDEN; i++)
    {
        for (j=0; j<NUM_HIDDEN; j++)
        {
            val = 0;
            for (k=0; k<bit_size; k++)
                if ((*b)[k+start_bit])
                    val += powers_of_two[bit_size - k - 1];
            f_val = val;
            f_val = (f_val / ((float)int_range))
                    * (MAX_VAL - MIN_VAL) + MIN_VAL;
            start_bit += bit_size;
            h_to_h[i][j] = f_val;
        }
    }

#endif

#ifdef USE_O_TO_H

    // output to hidden weights:
    for (i=0; i<NUM_OUTPUTS; i++)
    {
        for (j=0; j<NUM_HIDDEN; j++)
        {
            val = 0;
            for (k=0; k<bit_size; k++)
                if ((*b)[k+start_bit])
                    val += powers_of_two[bit_size - k - 1];
            f_val = val;
            f_val = (f_val / ((float)int_range))
                    * (MAX_VAL - MIN_VAL) + MIN_VAL;
            start_bit += bit_size;
            o_to_h[i][j] = f_val;
        }
    }

#endif
    // hidden to output weights:
    for (i=0; i<NUM_HIDDEN; i++)
    {
        for (j=0; j<NUM_OUTPUTS; j++)
        {
            val = 0;
            for (k=0; k<bit_size; k++)
                if ((*b)[k+start_bit])
                    val += powers_of_two[bit_size - k - 1];
            f_val = val;
            f_val = (f_val / ((float)int_range))
                    * (MAX_VAL - MIN_VAL) + MIN_VAL;
            start_bit += bit_size;
            h_to_o[i][j] = f_val;
        }
    }
}
```

```
//
//          Member function copy_float_weights_to_bits
//
//          This function converts a set of recurrent neural network
//          weights into a chromosome bit-vector.
//

void var_genetic_recurrent_network::
          copy_float_weights_to_bits(int population_index)
{
    bit_vector *bv = population[population_index];
    int start_bit = 0;
    int i, j, k;

    // input to hidden weights:
    for (i=0; i<NUM_INPUTS; i++)
    {
        for (j=0; j<NUM_HIDDEN; j++)
        {
            int i_val =
              ((float)int_range)*(i_to_h[i][j] - MIN_VAL)/(MAX_VAL - MIN_VAL);
            for (k=0; k<bit_size; k++)
                if (powers_of_two[bit_size - k - 1] & i_val)
                    *bv += (start_bit + k);
                else
                    *bv -= (start_bit + k);
            start_bit += bit_size;
        }
    }

#ifdef USE_I_TO_O

    // input to output weights:
    for (i=0; i<NUM_INPUTS; i++)
    {
        for (j=0; j<NUM_OUTPUTS; j++)
        {
            int i_val =
              ((float)int_range)*(i_to_o[i][j] - MIN_VAL)/(MAX_VAL - MIN_VAL);

            for (k=0; k<bit_size; k++)
                if (powers_of_two[bit_size - k - 1] & i_val)
                    (*bv) += (start_bit + k);
                else
                    (*bv) -= (start_bit + k);
            start_bit += bit_size;
        }
    }

#endif

#ifdef USE_H_TO_H

    // hidden to hidden weights:
    for (i=0; i<NUM_HIDDEN; i++)
    {
        for (j=0; j<NUM_HIDDEN; j++)
        {
            int i_val =
              ((float)int_range)*(h_to_h[i][j] - MIN_VAL)/(MAX_VAL - MIN_VAL);

            for (k=0; k<bit_size; k++)
```

```
                        if (powers_of_two[bit_size - k - 1] & i_val)
                            (*bv) += (start_bit + k);
                        else
                            (*bv) -= (start_bit + k);
                    start_bit += bit_size;
            }
        }

    #endif

    #ifdef USE_O_TO_H

        // output to hidden weights:
        for (i=0; i<NUM_OUTPUTS; i++)
        {
            for (j=0; j<NUM_HIDDEN; j++)
            {
                int i_val =
                  ((float)int_range)*(o_to_h[i][j] - MIN_VAL)/(MAX_VAL - MIN_VAL);

                for (k=0; k<bit_size; k++)
                    if (powers_of_two[bit_size - k - 1] & i_val)
                        (*bv) += (start_bit + k);
                    else
                        (*bv) -= (start_bit + k);
                start_bit += bit_size;
            }
        }

    #endif
        // hidden to output weights:
        for (i=0; i<NUM_HIDDEN; i++)
        {
            for (j=0; j<NUM_OUTPUTS; j++)
            {
                int i_val =
                  ((float)int_range)*(h_to_o[i][j] - MIN_VAL)/(MAX_VAL - MIN_VAL);

                for (k=0; k<bit_size; k++)
                    if (powers_of_two[bit_size - k - 1] & i_val)
                        (*bv) += (start_bit + k);
                    else
                        (*bv) -= (start_bit + k);
                start_bit += bit_size;
            }
        }
    }


    //
    //          Member function initialize_population
    //

    void var_genetic_recurrent_network::initialize_population()
    {
        for (int i=0; i<POPULATION; i++)
        {
            for (int j=0; j<NUM_bits_per_chromosome; j++)
            {
                int index = ran_seq.rndINT(0, num_bits_per_chromosome - 1);
                (*population[i]) += index;
            }
        }
    }
```

```
//
//            Member function sort_by_fitness
//
//            Note: I use a "bubble sort" here.  This is not efficient
//                  for very large populations as the sort time is
//                  O(number of chromosomes squared)
//

void var_genetic_recurrent_network::sort_by_fitness()
{
    float x;
    bit_vector *b;
    for (int i=0; i<POPULATION; i++)
    {
        for (int j=(POPULATION - 2); j>=i; j--)
        {
            if (fitnesses[j] > fitnesses[j+1])
            {
                x = fitnesses[j];
                b = population[j];
                fitnesses[j] = fitnesses[j+1];
                population[j] = population[j+1];
                fitnesses[j+1] = x;
                population[j+1] = b;
            }
        }
    }
#if 0
    cerr << "fitnesses: ";
    for (i=0; i<POPULATION; i++) cerr << fitnesses[i] << " ";
    cerr << "\n";
#endif
}


//
//            Member function solve
//
//            This function modifies the population with genetic
//            crossovers and mutation. It then uses the application-
//            specific fitness function to rate the fitness of each
//            chromosome in the new population.
//

float var_genetic_recurrent_network::solve()
{
    int i = 0, j;
    for (j=3*POPULATION/4 + 1; j<POPULATION; j++)
    {   // copy chromosome # i to # j:
        for (int k=0; k<NUM_bits_per_chromosome; k++)
        {
            if ((*population[i])[k])
                (*population[j]) += k;
            else
                (*population[j]) -= k;
        }
        i++;
        if (i >= (POPULATION/4 + 1))  i = 0;
    }

    // crossovers:
    for (j=0; j<POPULATION/5; j++)
    {
        int chrom_1 = ran_seq.rndINT(POPULATION/10+1, POPULATION - 1);
        int chrom_2 = ran_seq.rndINT(POPULATION/10+1, POPULATION - 1);
```

```
    int crossover_location =
        ran_seq.rndINT(1,num_bits_per_chromosome/bit_size);
    crossover_location *= bit_size;
    for (int k=0; k<crossover_location; k++)
    {
        int save = (*population[chrom_2])[k];
        if ((*population[chrom_1])[k])
            (*population[chrom_2]) += k;
        else
            (*population[chrom_2]) -= k;
        if (save)
            (*population[chrom_1]) += k;
        else
            (*population[chrom_1]) -= k;
    }
    i++;
}

// mutations:

for (j=5; j<POPULATION; j++)
{
    if (ran_seq.rndFP(0.0, 100.0) < 10.0)
    {
        int location = ran_seq.rndINT(0, num_bits_per_chromosome - 1);
        if ((*population[j])[location])
            (*population[j]) -= location;
        else
            (*population[j]) += location;
    }
}

// very high mutations for 1/8 of the population:

for (j=7*POPULATION/8; j<POPULATION; j++)
{
    for (int m=0; m<NUM_bits_per_chromosome/4+2; m++)
    {
        if (ran_seq.rndFP(0.0, 100.0) < 75.0)
        {
            int location = ran_seq.rndINT(0, num_bits_per_chromosome - 1);
            if ((*population[j])[location])
                (*population[j]) -= location;
            else
                (*population[j]) += location;
        }
    }
}

// Heuristic: I have noticed that sometimes there is a block
// of highly rated (by the fitness function), identical
// chromosomes at the beginning of the population list. The
// following check simply mutates any identical chromosomes
// so that we do not waste time evaluating identical members
// of the population:

for (i=0; i<POPULATION-1; i++)
{
    for (j=i+1; j<POPULATION; j++)
    {
        if ((*population[i]) == ((*population[j])))
        {
            int mutation_location =
                ran_seq.rndINT(0, num_bits_per_chromosome - 1);
```

```
                    if ((*population[j])[mutation_location])
                        (*population[j]) -= mutation_location;
                    else
                        (*population[j]) += mutation_location;
                }
            }
        }

    // Evaluate the fitness values of all chromosomes in the population:
    for (i=0; i<POPULATION; i++)
    {
        copy_bit_weights_to_floats(i);
        fitnesses[i] = fitness();
    }
    sort_by_fitness();

    // DEBUG printout:
#if 0
    for (i=0; i<POPULATION; i++)
    {
        cerr << "\nchrom: ";
        for (j=0; j<NUM_bits_per_chromosome; j++)
            cerr << (*population[i])[j] << " ";
    }
    cerr << "\n";
#endif

    return fitnesses[0];
}

//
//          Member function propagate
//
//          This function does not directly use any chromosomes
//          in the current population.  It is used to propagate the
//          current input-neuron activation values through the network
//          using the current weight set (as defined by member function
//          copy_bit_weights_to_floats for a specified chromosome).
//

void var_genetic_recurrent_network::propagate()
{
    for (int h=0; h<NUM_HIDDEN; h++)
    {
        hidden[h] = 0.0;
#ifdef USE_H_TO_H
        hidden_sums[h] = 0.0;
#endif
    }

#ifdef USE_H_TO_H
    for (int cycle=0; cycle<3; cycle++)
#endif
    {
        for (h=0; h<NUM_HIDDEN; h++)
        {
            for (int i=0; i<NUM_INPUTS; i++)
            {
                hidden[h] += inputs[i] * i_to_h[i][h];
            }
#ifdef USE_H_TO_H
            for (int h2=0; h2<NUM_HIDDEN; h2++)
            {
                hidden_sums[h] += hidden[h2] * h_to_h[h2][h];
```

```
                }
#endif
#ifdef USE_O_TO_H
            for (int o2=0; o2<NUM_OUTPUTS; o2++)
            {
                hidden_sums[h] += outputs[o2] * o_to_h[o2][h];
            }
#endif

#ifndef USE_H_TO_H
            hidden[h] = sigmoid(hidden[h]);
#else
            hidden[h] = sigmoid(hidden_sums[h]);
#endif
        }

        for (int o=0; o<NUM_OUTPUTS; o++)
            outputs[o] = 0.0;
        for (o=0; o<NUM_OUTPUTS; o++)
        {
            for (h=0; h<NUM_HIDDEN; h++)
            {
                outputs[o] += hidden[h] * h_to_o[h][o];
            }

#ifdef USE_I_TO_O
            for (int i=0; i<NUM_INPUTS; i++)
            {
                outputs[o] += inputs[i] * i_to_o[i][o];
            }
#endif
        }
        for (o=0; o<NUM_OUTPUTS; o++)
        {
            outputs[o] = sigmoid(outputs[o]);
        }
    }
}

//
//          Member function train
//
//          This function creates a specific number of new
//          generations in the population and uses member
//          function solve to evaluate each chromosome in each
//          population.
//

float var_genetic_recurrent_network::train(int num_generations)
{
    float best_error;
    for (int i=0; i<NUM_generations; i++)
    {
        best_error = solve();
        cerr << "current best error =" << best_error << "\n";
    }
    return best_error;
}


// APPLICATION-SPECIFIC FITNESS FUNCTION:

inline float val_sq(float x)
{
```

```
        return x * x;
}

int debug = 0;

#ifdef DO_ROTATION
float var_genetic_recurrent_network::fitness()
{
    static float in_1[]   = { 0.4, -0.4, -0.4, -0.4};
    static float in_2[]   = {-0.4,  0.4, -0.4, -0.4};
    static float in_3[]   = {-0.4, -0.4,  0.4, -0.4};
    static float in_4[]   = {-0.4, -0.4, -0.4,  0.4};
    static float out_1[]  = {-0.4, -0.4, -0.4,  0.4};
    static float out_2[]  = { 0.4, -0.4, -0.4, -0.4};
    static float out_3[]  = {-0.4,  0.4, -0.4, -0.4};
    static float out_4[]  = {-0.4, -0.4,  0.4, -0.4};

    float error = 0.0;
    for (int i=0; i<4; i++)
    {
        inputs[0] = in_1[i];
        inputs[1] = in_2[i];
        inputs[2] = in_3[i];
        inputs[3] = in_4[i];
        propagate();
        error += val_sq(outputs[0] - out_1[i]);
        error += val_sq(outputs[1] - out_2[i]);
        error += val_sq(outputs[2] - out_3[i]);
        error += val_sq(outputs[3] - out_4[i]);
        if (debug)
        {
            cerr << "inputs: " << inputs[0] << ", " << inputs[1]
                 << ", " << inputs[2] << ", " << inputs[3]
                 << "  outputs: " << outputs[0] << ", " << outputs[1]
                 << ", " << outputs[2] << ", " << outputs[3] << "\n";
        }
    }
//    cerr << "RMS error =" << error << "\n";
    return sqrt(error);
}
#endif


#ifdef DO_XOR

//              XOR test problem setup:

float var_genetic_recurrent_network::fitness()
{
    // test with a fitness for xor function:
    static float in_1[] = {-0.41, -0.4,   0.4,   0.4};
    static float in_2[] = {-0.4,   0.42, -0.4,   0.4};
    static float out[]  = {-0.401, 0.41,  0.39, -0.392};

    float error = 0.0;
    for (int i=0; i<4; i++)
    {
        inputs[0] = in_1[i];
        inputs[1] = in_2[i];
        propagate();
        error += val_sq(outputs[0] - out[i]);
        if (debug)
        {
            cerr << "inputs: " << inputs[0] << ", " << inputs[1]
```

```
                    << "  output: " << outputs[0] << "\n";
            }
        }
 //    cerr << "RMS error =" << error << "\n";
        return sqrt(error);
    }
#endif


#ifdef DO_ANT

const int NUM_ANT_CYCLES = 30;

float var_genetic_recurrent_network::fitness()
{

    float error = 8;   // represents eight uneaten pieces of ant food

    // Initial environment for the ant:
    int current_x = 0; // ant's starting grid position
    int current_y = 3;

    // direction values: 1=up, 2=right, 3=down, 4=left
    // (looking at Figure 12.3)
    int current_direction = 2;

    int grid[8][8];
    for (int i=0; i<8; i++)
        for (int j=0; j<8; j++)
            grid[i][j] = 0;
    // Initial ant food locations on the grid:
    grid[1][3] = grid[2][4] = grid[2][5] = grid[3][5] = 1;
    grid[5][5] = grid[6][4] = grid[6][3] = grid[6][1] = 1;

    // Initial sensor values:
    inputs[0] =  0.3; // food in the square in front of the ant
    inputs[1] = -0.3; // no wall in front of the ant

    int eating_flag = 0;

    // Output codes:
    //
    //     Highest output neuron      meaning
    //     --------------------       -------
    //
    //                         0      move forward
    //                         1      turn to the left
    //                         2      turn to the right
    //

    for (i=0; i<NUM_ANT_CYCLES; i++)
    {
        eating_flag = 0;
        propagate();
        // Find the largest output-neuron value:
        int max_index = 0;
        float max_val = outputs[0];
        for (int m=1; m<NUM_OUTPUTS; m++)
        {
            if (max_val < outputs[m])
            {
                max_val = outputs[m];
                max_index = m;
            }
        }
```

```
        }

        switch (max_index)
        {
            case 0:   // move forward
                switch(current_direction)
                {
                    case 1:  // up (y coordinate increases)
                        if (current_y <= 6)  current_y++;
                        break;
                    case 2:  // right (x coordinate increases)
                        if (current_x <= 6)  current_x++;
                        break;
                    case 3:  // down (y coordinate decreases)
                        if (current_y > 0)  current_y-;
                        break;
                    case 4:  // left (x coordinate decreases)
                        if (current_x > 0) current_x-;
                        break;
                }
                if (grid[current_x][current_y] != 0)
                {
                    error -= 1;
                    grid[current_x][current_y] = 0; // cannot eat food twice!
                    if (debug)
                    {
                        eating_flag = 1;
                    }
                }
                break;
            case 1: // turn left
                current_direction -= 1;
                if (current_direction < 1) current_direction = 1;
                break;
            case 2: // turn right
                current_direction  += 1;
                if (current_direction > 4) current_direction = 4;
                break;
        }

#ifdef DEBUG
        if (debug)
        {
            cerr << "in: " << inputs[0] << ", " << inputs[1]
                 << "  out: " << outputs[0] << ", " << outputs[1]
                 << ", " << outputs[2] << "\n";
        }
#endif

        // Set input-neuron sensors for the next iteration:

        inputs[0] = inputs[1] = -0.3;
        int next_x = current_x;
        int next_y = current_y;
        switch (current_direction)
        {
            case 1: // up
                if (current_y <= 6)
                {
                    next_y += 1;
                } else
                {
                    inputs[1] = +0.3; // path blocked by boundary
                }
```

```
                break;
            case 2: // right
                if (current_x <= 6)
                {
                    next_x += 1;
                } else
                {
                    inputs[1] = +0.3; // path blocked by boundary
                }
                break;
            case 3: // down
                if (current_y >= 1)
                {
                    next_y -= 1;
                } else
                {
                    inputs[1] = +0.3; // path blocked by boundary
                }
                break;
            case 4: // left
                if (current_x >= 1)
                {
                    next_x -= 1;
                } else
                {
                    inputs[1] = +0.3; // path blocked by boundary
                }
                break;
        }
        if (grid[next_x][next_y] != 0)
            inputs[0] = +0.3; // food directly in front of the ant
        if (debug)
        {
            if (eating_flag == 0)
                cerr << "  (" << current_x << ", " << current_y << ")    ";
            else
                cerr << " <[" << current_x << ", " << current_y << "]>  ";
            if (((i+1)/5)*5 == (i+1))  cerr << "\n";
        }

    }
    if (debug)  cerr << "\n\n";

 //   cerr << "RMS error =" << error << "\n";
    return error;
}
#endif


void main()
{
    var_genetic_recurrent_network v2(12);
    int generation_count = 0;
    cerr << "Starting...\n";
    for (int chrome_size=4; chrome_size<12; chrome_size++)
    {
        if (chrome_size > 4)
        {
            cerr << "\n\nCHANGING CHROMOSOME SIZE TO "
                << chrome_size << "\n";
            debug = 0;
            v2.change_chromosome_size(chrome_size);
        }
```

```
for (int iter=0; iter<10; iter++)
{
    debug = 0;
    v2.train(10);
    generation_count += 10;
    debug = 1;
    v2.copy_bit_weights_to_floats(0); //should be the best one!
    cerr << "\n\ngeneration " << generation_count << "\n";
    v2.fitness();
}
    }
}
```

12.4.1 Example execution for the bit-rotation problem

I now vary the chromosome size from four bits to twelve bits. The chromosome size increases by one bit every hundred generations. The following output at generation 70 uses four-bit chromosomes:

```
generation 70
inputs: 0.4, -0.4, -0.4, -0.4   outputs: -0.499711, 0.372195, -0.497502, -0.477827
inputs: -0.4, 0.4, -0.4, -0.4   outputs: -0.492075, -0.499305, 0.018738, -0.49976
inputs: -0.4, -0.4, 0.4, -0.4   outputs: -0.479713, -0.499332, -0.019361, 0.341974
inputs: -0.4, -0.4, -0.4, 0.4   outputs: 0.290176, -0.497342, -0.482847, -0.367496
current best error =0.627585
```

The following listing shows the test cases with the best set of weights that the genetic algorithm has found after 100 generations. The chromosome size increases by one bit per weight every hundred generations.

```
current best error =0.627585
current best error =0.627585
current best error =0.627585


generation 100
inputs: 0.4, -0.4, -0.4, -0.4   outputs: -0.499711, 0.372195, -0.497502, -0.477827
inputs: -0.4, 0.4, -0.4, -0.4   outputs: -0.492075, -0.499305, 0.018738, -0.49976
inputs: -0.4, -0.4, 0.4, -0.4   outputs: -0.479713, -0.499332, -0.019361, 0.341974
inputs: -0.4, -0.4, -0.4, 0.4   outputs: 0.290176, -0.497342, -0.482847, -0.367496


CHANGING CHROMOSOME SIZE TO 5
current best error =0.513794
current best error =0.513794
```

The following listing shows the test set for the best weights after 400 generations.

```
current best error =0.335974
current best error =0.335974


generation 400
inputs: 0.4, -0.4, -0.4, -0.4   outputs: -0.496174, 0.329423, -0.494836, -0.402841
inputs: -0.4, 0.4, -0.4, -0.4   outputs: -0.494657, -0.435507, 0.272012, -0.499992
inputs: -0.4, -0.4, 0.4, -0.4   outputs: -0.454326, -0.426427, -0.395056, 0.227802
```

```
inputs: -0.4, -0.4, -0.4, 0.4  outputs: 0.386688, -0.487016, -0.392997, -0.290815


CHANGING CHROMOSOME SIZE TO 8
current best error =0.335974
```

The following listing shows the test cases evaluated for the best set of weights found in generation number 800:

```
current best error =0.273584
current best error =0.273584
current best error =0.273584


generation 800
inputs: 0.4, -0.4, -0.4, -0.4  outputs: -0.494789, 0.397439, -0.495642, -0.277663
inputs: -0.4, 0.4, -0.4, -0.4  outputs: -0.491387, -0.451681, 0.386519, -0.499886
inputs: -0.4, -0.4, 0.4, -0.4  outputs: -0.421197, -0.394948, -0.457371, 0.467196
inputs: -0.4, -0.4, -0.4, 0.4  outputs: 0.449362, -0.490101, -0.359126, -0.40739
```

12.4.2 Example execution for the XOR problem

I again vary the chromosome size from four bits to twelve bits. The chromosome size increases by one every hundred generations. The following output at generation 30 uses four-bit chromosomes:

```
current best error =0.785164
current best error =0.785164
current best error =0.785011
current best error =0.783092
current best error =0.781111
current best error =0.780286
current best error =0.780286


generation 30
inputs: -0.41, -0.4  output: -0.04252
inputs: -0.4, 0.42  output: -0.019991
inputs: 0.4, -0.4  output: 0.042688
inputs: 0.4, 0.4  output: 0.026116
current best error =0.780261
current best error =0.780261
current best error =0.780261
current best error =0.780232
```

Notice that at generation 30, the classification for the input values $(0.4, 0.4)$ is incorrect. This is the input combination for the XOR problem that is difficult for a neural network to learn.

At generation 50, the neural network starts to correctly classify all test cases:

```
generation 50
inputs: -0.41, -0.4  output: -0.015871
inputs: -0.4, 0.42  output: 0.002975
inputs: 0.4, -0.4  output: 0.023758
inputs: 0.4, 0.4  output: -0.008513
```

```
current best error =0.771485
current best error =0.771412
current best error =0.77109
current best error =0.770525
current best error =0.770508
current best error =0.770508
```

The network with the best set of weights produced by the genetic algorithm classifies all patterns if we "increase the contrast" and consider every negative output value to be a Boolean FALSE and every positive output value to be a Boolean TRUE. The network is not yet reliably trained, however.

```
CHANGING CHROMOSOME SIZE TO 5
current best error =0.771459
current best error =0.771459
current best error =0.771459
current best error =0.771459
current best error =0.770369
current best error =0.770369
current best error =0.770369
current best error =0.770369
current best error =0.770369
current best error =0.770369


generation 110
inputs: -0.41, -0.4  output: 0.007971
inputs: -0.4, 0.42  output: 0.044338
inputs: 0.4, -0.4  output: 0.019696
inputs: 0.4, 0.4  output: -0.038939
current best error =0.770369
```

In this listing, notice that the error for the best set of weights produced by the genetic algorithm increased slightly when the chromosome size changed, and it takes a few generations to catch up to the lowest error value from the previous chromosome size.

```
inputs: -0.4, 0.42  output: 0.035664
inputs: 0.4, -0.4  output: 0.049256
inputs: 0.4, 0.4  output: -0.00131
current best error =0.734929
current best error =0.734929
current best error =0.734929
current best error =0.734929
current best error =0.734929
current best error =0.734929
current best error =0.734929
current best error =0.734929
current best error =0.734929
current best error =0.734929


generation 400
inputs: -0.41, -0.4  output: -0.038717
inputs: -0.4, 0.42  output: 0.035664
inputs: 0.4, -0.4  output: 0.049256
inputs: 0.4, 0.4  output: -0.00131
```

```
CHANGING CHROMOSOME SIZE TO 8
current best error =0.734094
```

The next listing shows test output from the best set of weight values found after 700 generations:

```
current best error =0.73182
current best error =0.73182
current best error =0.73182


generation 700
inputs: -0.41, -0.4  output: -0.02595
inputs: -0.4, 0.42   output: 0.04692
inputs: 0.4, -0.4   output: 0.041777
inputs: 0.4, 0.4   output: -0.01542


CHANGING CHROMOSOME SIZE TO 11
current best error =0.731715
current best error =0.731715
```

The performance of the network slowly improves. Since the network required to solve the XOR problem is a simple, nonrecurrent, three-layer network, for practical applications we would use the C++ classes developed in Chapter 9, which use backward error propagation.

12.4.3 Two example executions for the artificial ant problem

After ten generations, the simulated ant has not learned to find food. The following listing shows x-y coordinates of the ant at each time step. Coordinates bracketed with <[ ]> indicate locations that contained food (which the ant eats immediately).

```
current best error =6
current best error =6


generation 10
 <[1, 3]>    (2, 3)     (3, 3)     (4, 3)     (5, 3)
 <[6, 3]>    (7, 3)     (7, 3)     (7, 4)     (7, 5)
  (7, 6)     (7, 7)     (7, 7)     (7, 7)     (7, 7)
  (7, 6)     (7, 5)     (7, 4)     (7, 3)     (7, 2)
  (7, 1)     (7, 0)     (7, 0)     (7, 0)     (7, 0)
  (6, 0)     (5, 0)     (4, 0)     (3, 0)     (2, 0)
```

The next listing shows a statistical anomaly! On rare occasions, a "lucky" mutation will find a good set of weights very quickly. By generation 40 (using only four bits per weight), we have found a very good set of weights (i.e., the weights program the ant to behave efficiently in its environment).

```
current best error =5
current best error =5
current best error =0
current best error =0
```

```
generation 40
 <[1, 3]>     (2, 3)      (2, 3)     <[2, 4]>   <[2, 5]>
  (2, 6)      (2, 6)      (2, 6)      (2, 6)     (2, 5)
  (2, 5)     <[3, 5]>     (4, 5)     <[5, 5]>    (6, 5)
  (6, 5)      (6, 5)      (6, 5)     <[6, 4]>   <[6, 3]>
  (6, 2)     <[6, 1]>     (6, 0)      (6, 0)     (6, 0)
  (6, 0)      (6, 0)      (6, 0)      (6, 0)     (6, 0)
```

Figure 12.10 shows the ant's trail after 40 generations.

The following set of listings shows another execution run of the ant simulation.

```
Starting...
current best error =6
current best error =6
current best error =6
current best error =6
current best error =6
current best error =6
current best error =6
current best error =6
current best error =6
current best error =6


generation 10
 <[1, 3]>     (2, 3)      (3, 3)      (4, 3)     (5, 3)
 <[6, 3]>     (7, 3)      (7, 3)      (7, 4)     (7, 5)
  (7, 6)      (7, 7)      (7, 7)      (7, 7)     (7, 7)
  (7, 7)      (7, 7)      (7, 7)      (7, 7)     (7, 7)
  (7, 7)      (7, 7)      (7, 7)      (7, 7)     (7, 7)
  (7, 7)      (7, 7)      (7, 7)      (7, 7)     (7, 7)
```

After 10 generations, the ant has not adapted to its environment. As seen in Figure 12.11, it gets stuck in a corner.

The next listing shows the behavior of the ant using the best set of weights in the chromosome population after 30 generations.

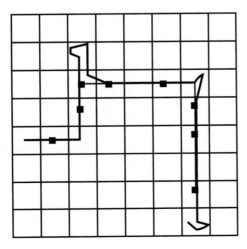

Figure 12.10 The ant has learned to find all of the food after 40 generations.

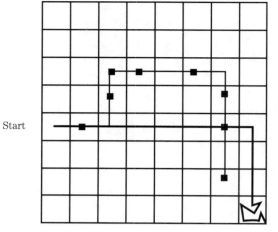

Start

Figure 12.11 After only 10 generations, the ant gets stuck in a corner.

```
current best error =5
current best error =5
current best error =3


generation 30
 <[1, 3]>    (2, 3)      (2, 3)     <[2, 4]>    <[2, 5]>
 (2, 5)     <[3, 5]>     (4, 5)     <[5, 5]>     (5, 5)
 (5, 5)      (5, 5)      (5, 5)      (5, 5)      (5, 5)
 (5, 5)      (5, 5)      (5, 5)      (5, 5)      (5, 5)
 (5, 5)      (5, 5)      (5, 5)      (5, 5)      (5, 5)
 (5, 5)      (5, 5)      (5, 5)      (5, 5)      (5, 5)
```

The next listing shows the behavior of the ant using the best set of weights in the chromosome population after 70 generations. The ant is still only finding five out of eight pieces of food.

```
current best error =3
current best error =3


generation 70
 <[1, 3]>    (2, 3)      (2, 3)      (2, 3)      (2, 3)
 <[2, 4]>   <[2, 5]>     (2, 5)     <[3, 5]>     (4, 5)
 <[5, 5]>    (5, 5)      (5, 5)      (5, 5)      (5, 5)
 (5, 5)      (5, 5)      (5, 5)      (5, 5)      (5, 5)
 (5, 5)      (5, 5)      (5, 5)      (5, 5)      (5, 5)
 (5, 5)      (5, 5)      (5, 5)      (5, 5)      (5, 5)
```

The next listing shows the behavior of the ant using the best set of weights in the chromosome population after 90 generations. The ant is now finding all eight pieces of food.

```
current best error =0
current best error =0
```

```
generation 90
 <[1, 3]>    (2, 3)      (2, 3)    <[2, 4]>    <[2, 5]>
 (2, 6)      (2, 6)      (2, 6)     (2, 6)      (2, 5)
 (2, 5)    <[3, 5]>      (4, 5)    <[5, 5]>     (6, 5)
 (6, 5)      (6, 5)      (6, 5)    <[6, 4]>    <[6, 3]>
 (6, 2)    <[6, 1]>      (6, 0)     (6, 0)      (6, 0)
 (6, 0)      (5, 0)      (5, 0)     (5, 0)      (5, 0)
```

After generation 90, I let the simulation run for another 10 generations to show the transition from using four bits per weight to using five bits per weight.

```
CHANGING CHROMOSOME SIZE TO 5
current best error =5
current best error =5
current best error =5
current best error =0
current best error =0
current best error =0
current best error =0
current best error =0
current best error =0
current best error =0
```

```
generation 110
 <[1, 3]>    (2, 3)      (2, 3)    <[2, 4]>    <[2, 5]>
 (2, 6)      (2, 6)      (2, 6)     (2, 6)      (2, 5)
 (2, 5)    <[3, 5]>      (4, 5)    <[5, 5]>     (6, 5)
 (6, 5)      (6, 5)      (6, 5)    <[6, 4]>    <[6, 3]>
 (6, 2)    <[6, 1]>      (6, 0)     (6, 0)      (6, 0)
 (6, 0)      (6, 0)      (6, 0)     (6, 0)      (5, 0)
```

Notice that the population lost the chromosome(s) that represented "perfect" (i.e., zero error for the ant simulation fitness function) weight sets. As usual, when the population is slightly "damaged" in the transition to using more bits per weight, the population quickly recovers.

Figure 12.12 shows the searching behavior that the ant has learned.

In experimenting with the three test problems and variable bit-length weights, I was surprised at the difference between "classical" neural network problems like bit rotation and XOR, and the ant learning simulation problem. From my experiments, encoding behavior patterns in the ant's neural pathways requires far fewer bits of information per connection-strength weight than the more traditional neural network problems.

12.5 Using Genetic Algorithms to Train Neural Networks

You have now seen two versions of an example program (with and without Vari-GenSearch™) solve three sample problems. Clearly, the sample programs do a poor job at training simple (nonrecurrent) neural networks compared with the backward error propagation techniques used in Chapter 9.

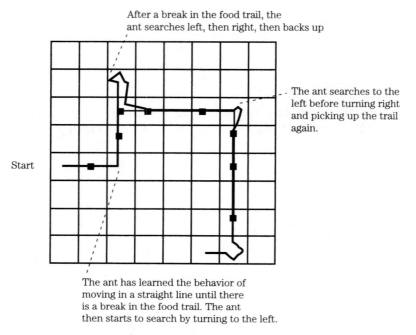

After a break in the food trail, the
ant searches left, then right, then backs up

.. The ant searches to the
left before turning right
and picking up the trail
again.

Start

The ant has learned the behavior of
moving in a straight line until there
is a break in the food trail. The ant
then starts to search by turning to the left.

Figure 12.12 The artificial ant has learned to follow a food trail.

Using genetic algorithms to train highly recurrent neural networks, however, looks promising. As this book goes to press, I am actively experimenting with this new technique. I want to share with you the directions that my own research is taking:

- Optimization of VariGenSearch™. The example programs in this chapter are my first experiments in genetically training neural networks. Further optimizations will include:

- Using additional neural network parameters like activation thresholds in the learning process.

- Using backward error propagation with genetic learning to decrease training times.

- Exploration of more exotic neural network structures. Most neural network simulations feature complete interconnections between neuron layers. I believe that the following techniques will provide practical neural networks for processing real time data:

- Starting with highly recurrent neural networks with complete interconnection between neuron layers. As part of the genetic algorithm fitness function, favoring members of the population with weights that have a zero value; these weights can be effectively removed from the network to produce networks that execute faster.

- Giving up the idea of segregating neurons into specified layers. Build network architectures with a uniform set of neurons. After specifying which of these neurons are input and output neurons, produce random connections. During training, the fitness function should prefer weight sets that have many zero-valued weights. This process could produce very sparse randomly-connected networks with adequate short-term memory to process time series data. I experimented with this type of network in 1987 while I was writing a commercial product for experimenting with neural networks. However, instead of using genetic learning, I used random training, so that only very small networks could be trained. I think that the combination of genetic algorithm learning of weight sets and randomly connected architectures will produce useful networks that are more similar to human neural networks.

Bibliography

Abelson, Harold and Sussman, Gerald 1985. *Structure and Interpretation of Computer Programs*. Cambridge, Massachusetts: MIT Press; New York: McGraw-Hill.

Constraint systems are one of many interesting topics covered in this book.

Booch, Grady 1991. *Object Oriented Design*. Redwood City, California: Benjamin/Cummings.

Excellent introduction to the object model of software development.

Goldberg, David 1989. *Genetic Algorithms*. Reading, Massachusetts: Addison-Wesley.

This is my favorite reference for genetic algorithms.

Koza, John 1993. *Genetic Programming*. Cambridge, Massachusetts: MIT Press.

Leler, William 1988. *Constraint Programming Languages*. New York: Addison-Wesley.

This book provides a good overview of constraint systems.

Rumelhart, David and McClelland, James 1986. *Parallel Distributed Processing*. Cambridge, Massachusetts: MIT Press.

Watson, Mark 1991. *Common LISP Modules. Artificial Intelligence in the Era of Neural Networks and Chaos Theory*. New York: Springer-Verlag.

Watson, Mark 1993. *Portable GUI Development with C++*. New York: McGraw-Hill.

This book contains GUI applications using neural networks and text indexing.

Index

Illustration are indicated by **boldface** numbers

ABOUT THE AUTHOR

Mark Watson is a computer scientist working with the Science Applications International Corporation and has experience with expert system tools, natural language processing, neural networks and systems programming, and programs in C++, C, LISP, Prolog, Smalltalk, and Pascal. He has been instrumental in the design and implementation of new technologies, such as the SAIC Object Programming Environment (SOPE), and in establishing the portability of these technologies. Watson is the author of *Portable GUI Development with C++*, also published by McGraw-Hill, Inc.

Other Bestsellers of Related Interest

OS/2 Extra!: VIO, KBD, and MOU Special Functions Revealed
—Edited by Len Dorfman and Marc J. Neuberger
This exclusive guide fills the gap in the official documentation for OS/2 2.0-2.1. Contains undocumented OS/2 keyboard, mouse, and video calls previously available only online.
0-8306-4567-5 $19.95 Paper

Instant OS/2®!: Porting C Applications to OS/2
—Len Dorfman
The secret to writing DOS applications that run under OS/2. Provides "common" named and prototyped C libraries for DOS and OS/2—complete program code furnished on disk. Supports OS/2 2.1, DOS 6.0, and Borland's new C++ for OS/2 compiler.
0-8306-4522-5 $34.95 Paper

Stacker® for OS/2® & DOS: An Illustrated Tutorial
—Lisa Heller
Everything the manual doesn't tell you about how to install, customize, use, and troubleshoot Stacker 3.0-3.1. Also reveals instant solutions to eight of the most common problems reported to the Stac OS/2 support staff.
0-07-027986-1 $19.95 Paper

OS/2® Connectivity and Networking: A Guide to Communications Manager/2
—John E. Johnston
Shows systems programmers and LAN administrators how to overcome problems associated with implementing OS/2 across the network using Communications Manager/2.
0-07-032696-7 $39.95 Paper

Writing OS/2® REXX Programs

—Ronny Richardson

The first book devoted solely to the OS/2 version of REXX. Explains how to go beyond batch files and take full advantage of the powerful REXX language. Disk included.

0-07-052372-X $39.95 Paper

The Ultimate OS/2® Programmer's Manual

—John Mueller

Reviewed for accuracy by IBM, this book has solutions to almost any problem programmers are likely to encounter when writing OS/2 applications.

0-07-043972-9 $36.95 Paper
0-07-043971-0 $45.00 Hard

How to Order

 Call 1-800-822-8158
24 hours a day,
7 days a week
in U.S. and Canada

 Mail this coupon to:
McGraw-Hill, Inc.
Blue Ridge Summit, PA
17294-0840

 Fax your order to:
717-794-5291

 EMAIL
70007.1531@COMPUSERVE.COM
COMPUSERVE: GO MH

Thank you for your order!

Shipping and Handling Charges

Order Amount	Within U.S.	Outside U.S.
Less than $15	$3.45	$5.25
$15.00 - $24.99	$3.95	$5.95
$25.00 - $49.99	$4.95	$6.95
$50.00 - and up	$5.95	$7.95

EASY ORDER FORM— SATISFACTION GUARANTEED

Ship to:

Name _____

Address _____

City/State/Zip _____

Daytime Telephone No. _____

ITEM NO.	QUANTITY	AMT.

Method of Payment:

☐ Check or money order enclosed (payable to McGraw-Hill)

☐ [Cards]   ☐ VISA

☐ MasterCard   ☐ DISCOVER

	Shipping & Handling charge from chart below
	Subtotal
Please add applicable state & local sales tax	
	TOTAL

Account No. ☐☐☐☐☐☐☐☐☐☐☐☐☐

Signature _____ Exp. Date _____
Order invalid without signature

In a hurry? Call 1-800-822-8158 anytime, day or night, or visit your local bookstore.

Code = BC44ZNA